THE FUN OF
OLD CARS

THE FUN OF OLD CARS

*Collecting and Restoring
Antique, Classic &
Special Interest Automobiles*

by BOB STUBENRAUCH

Photographs by the author

DODD, MEAD & COMPANY · NEW YORK

The author wishes to express his thanks to Doubleday & Company, Inc. for permission to reprint seven lines from THE GREEN HAT by Michael Arlen; Simon & Schuster, Inc. for material from THE BOY IN THE MODEL T by Stephen Longstreet; and Harper & Row, Publishers for the quotation from A HISTORY OF THE WORLD'S CLASSIC CARS by Richard Hough and Michael Frostick.

LIBRARY OF CONGRESS CATALOG CARD NUMBER: 67-25110

PRINTED IN THE UNITED STATES OF AMERICA

FOR LEAH, DAVID, AND BRUCE

ACKNOWLEDGMENTS

I wish to thank the following for their generous cooperation.

Edward Berry, owner and restorer of the 1900 Locomobile. Harold R. Kraft, owner and restorer of the 1908 Sears Auto Buggy. Joseph Thamm, owner and restorer of the 1908 Jackson. Lester Cutting, owner, and Walter McCarthy, restorer of the 1910 Courier Speedster. (Mr. McCarthy is also the owner and restorer of the 1911 Panhard and Lavassor). Robert Zlotoff, owner and restorer of the 1911 Kelsey Motorette. Charles Hartman, owner and restorer of the 1912 Case and 1914 Benz. L. P. Jorgensen, owner of the 1913 Detroit Electric. My thanks also to William W. Willock, Jr., former owner of the Detroit Electric. Richard A. Knies, owner and restorer of the 1914 Rolls Royce Silver Ghost coupe. John Sammons, owner and restorer of the 1920 Model T Ford. John Lindhardt, owner of the 1926 Packard, 1934 Packard twelve and co-owner of the 1937 Buick Roadmaster. Joseph Gaeta, owner and restorer of the 1927 Isotta-Fraschini. Gustav Magnuson, owner of the 1929 Hispano-Suiza. Philip Wichard, owner and restorer of the 1931 LaSalle roadster. Mr. Wichard is also the owner of the 1931 Rolls-Royce Phantom II cabriolet and the Town and Country Chrysler. Donald Gilbert, owner and restorer of the 1931 Pierce Arrow and co-owner of the 1937 Buick Roadmaster. Edward Stolarcyk, owner of the 1934 Duesenberg restored by Russell Strauch. Harold Hauser, owner of the 1937 Cord 812 restored by John Longo. Jackson Bailey, owner and restorer of the 1941 Lincoln Continental coupe. William R. Evans, owner and restorer of the 1929 Ford Model A station wagon. Captain Robert Snowden, Jr., owner and restorer of the 1935 Ford V-8 phaeton.

I would also like to thank Henry Genn, Robert Gold, Warren Kraft, Charles Willmore of J. S. Inskip-New York, Lucy and Richard Waldman, John Stubenrauch, Joseph Morgenthaler and Mr. and Mrs. Jacob Goodman for their kind assistance. A special note of thanks is due my wife, without whose encouragement and aid this book could not have been done.

BOB STUBENRAUCH

CONTENTS

CONTENTS

FOREWORD

It is hard for me to determine just when I became ensnared by the magic and mystery of grand old automobiles. As a child, I picked blackberries along the route of the Motor Parkway, Long Island's early toll road for the motoring gentry. Once in an hour or two, the drowsy summer silence would be broken by a mounting roar, and a dusty, snarling Lincoln, Cord or Packard would speed by high on the banked curves. Not so many years later I took a short cut through the rear ranks of a used car lot, on my way to high school. It seemed incredible to me then that here they were, unwanted and unsalable, a V-16 Marmon, a Pierce roadster and a Packard twelve. In 1941 no one wanted a thirsty Marmon even for the three hundred dollars whitewashed on its windshield. At that time I carried in my wallet pictures of the new Continental and the 812 Cord and heatedly debated with my classmates which was the most glorious car ever designed.

That debate still breaks out anew. It is the aim of this book to acquaint the antique and classic car enthusiast, both novice and old hand, with a detailed photographic scrutiny of some grand old automobiles. They include well-known cars, little-known cars, and cars undeservedly unknown. I hope the reader will feel after completing this work that he has seen each machine for himself and has been provided with fresh fuel for further happy argument in this most exciting of hobbies!

BOB STUBENRAUCH

A typical Long Island car meet.

1. HOW TO FIND
AN ANTIQUE CAR

THE antique car virus usually sneaks up on the victim in deceptively innocuous ways. You may find yourself trailing a caravan of old-timers to a Sunday meet, your planned picnic postponed. The smell of brass polish and old leather, the old-fashioned aspect of the machines and the throaty muttering of the big-bore cylinders may ensnare you then and there. If you are a hold-out, you might settle for hanging a few antique car prints in your den. Then perhaps another visit to a meet or a movie like *Genevieve* or *The Great Race* will persuade you that being a once-in-a-while spectator is not enough. A participant you must be!

At the point when you first consider buying an antique or classic car, you are apt to be discouraged by the apparent wealth of problems. This is a hobby unlike most others. You can walk into any large department store and become outfitted as an active stamp or coin collector. If you like airplanes, you can find kits in every size for models of virtually every plane ever flown. Try walking into the largest hobby shop in your state and requesting a 1915 Model T roadster fully equipped and no rust, please. Before they carry you off forcibly, you will realize that this is not really a prosaic public hobby but an intensely personal one pursued by people in a happy state of near mania. It is therefore fair to say that no routine way exists to acquire just the particular old car you desire.

In seeking out an old car, two paths to that end will soon become apparent. The cars found through the first path will be those belonging to other antique car buffs. Whether restored or not, their possibilities will have been explored by someone aware of their interest and value. Here the element of personal discovery is lacking, and there is the completely different price scale to be consid-

3

ered. The going price for a discovered car will be substantially more than the one the farmer put on the hopeless wreck he was happy to eject from his barn.

Aside from the mundane matter of money, what makes the second path so appealing is the challenge of being the first to find and appreciate a distinctive old automobile. The dream of tramping down weeds, prying open weathered doors sagging on rusty hinges and then speculating on what you could do with that huge old tourer under the dust of five decades is a unique thrill.

Before you arrive at the key decision to shop for a "known" automobile or to scour the backwoods for an original discovery, you should consider these factors: Are you interested in doing a full restoration from a veritable hulk, or are you more inclined to buy a restored machine which you can immediately take to the road? If you have limited time to devote to the full restoration or even partial restoration of an old-timer, you should look for a car already put in good condition. Any undiscovered car you might find would undoubtedly require more time than you can spare. However, no true antique car enthusiast can fail to follow up any leads that come his way. You should always keep in mind that a rare Pierce Arrow in derelict condition might be swapped for a Packard sedan in mint condition. Many owners have found, acquired and swapped their way up the ladder to possess a car they would have been unable to purchase initially.

A hard look at your capabilities would be in order at this time. You might start by noting your assets and liabilities.

Mechanical Skills: What have you done around modern cars? Have you changed plugs, tuned an engine? Have you rebuilt a carburetor, relined the brake drums? Do you have skills in your job that are closely allied, such as machine shop, automobile or aircraft factory experience. Remember, anything you can't do well yourself will have to be jobbed out. If it is any consolation, few restorers, however expert, do everything on their cars. Tops for the great tourers, wooden-spoked wheels and upholstery work are usually left to specialists. The value of belonging to the appropriate club is impossible to overstate. This is where the specialists in your area are found and where you can get expert help and advice. Naturally, the cost of restoration will soar if you are unable to handle any of the work. It is easy to spend four or five thousand dollars for the work on a major rebuild at the prevailing rate of three to five dollars an hour for skilled labor.

Work Space: It goes without saying that you cannot own an antique or classic car without a garage to keep it in. If your garage is the skimpy ten-by-twenty-foot size beloved by builders in today's suburbia, you will have a prob-

This 1939 Cadillac five-passenger coupe is rated a full classic. Body is by Fleet-wood. A missing rear seat and minor rust in lower panels were the only flaws in this car offered for $350 in 1961.

lem to do more than store your vehicle. Ideally, a garage with space for a work bench and room to remove and work on major parts, such as fenders, would be the car-and-a-half or two-car size. Overhead beams to support a chain hoist for engine removal or body removal are certainly useful.

Practical Usage: Surprisingly enough, this aspect of old car ownership is overlooked by many. A Ford Model T speedster, which is basically an engine, two bucket seats and a gas tank on a light chassis, would hardly be suitable for a family of four or five. The choice of a small two-seater or a big tourer or sedan will depend to some extent on how many in the family will engage in tours and meet trips. If you intend to own more than one antique or classic, this question becomes academic.

Available Time: The amount of time you expect to devote to your project, without becoming a social outcast, will enter into your final selection of a vehicle. If you have, say, one afternoon a weekend free and the relic that has fired your imagination is in need of total restoration, you should count on at least a year of work. This is an area where predictions are dangerous. You may be stumped for six months for a small but vital part or you might find a "parts car" with the items you need in better condition than those on your own automobile.

Cold Hard Cash: The plenitude of this last item will affect several of the previous elements in planning your old car restoration project. With a comfortable check book and a stack of club bulletins with their columns of classified ads at hand, many steps in the restoration project can be accelerated fantastically. Even for the few with unlimited funds, however, half the fun is

The novice old-car buff will have to accustom himself to examining cars in this condition. Actually this Buick is restorable.

prowling about the old car flea markets and wrecking yards for the elusive parts needed.

At this point you have an idea of how much time, space and money you wish to devote to the old beast you hope to find. You have looked into the trials of actual restoration work, perhaps joined a local old car club and visited other members at work on their automobiles. After the decision to go ahead in your search has been made, let us say, in favor of known cars from sources within one or two hundred miles of your home, one last precaution should be taken: Acquire up-to-the-minute information about the going market price of the car you are looking for. If you are shopping for a Model T or an A, this is fairly simple. If you come across a Stoddard-Dayton or a Moon or a Metz and have no idea of its relative worth, get help fast. A small binder holding your find for a few days will enable you to research the car in the appropriate club and avoid overpaying.

Armed with some idea of your dream car's worth you are ready to start looking. First, communicate with the regional branches of the major clubs in your area. The Antique Auto Club of America, The Horseless Carriage Club of America or The Classic Car Club of America might lead you to cars for sale among their members. Most meets produce several cars for sale by hobbyists who are anxious to start that next project. Talk to people at these outings and tell them just what you are looking for. Some years back a well-known collector, with several fellow hobbyists and a car trailer in tow, would spend a weekend systematically combing one small area of New England. If you have the time, this approach might pay off, although nothing is more depressing than to speak to a farmer reached by five miles of the most inaccessible roads in creation and then to be regaled with tales of the six other car collectors he has seen in the last year.

You will greatly increase your chances of making a find if you have a platoon of agents working for you. I hasten to add that these agents would not be the paid experts some millionaire collectors employ. You might start by simply advising your relatives and friends, particularly those who travel out in the country, that you want to buy an old automobile. Then you might go to several real estate brokers in the distant suburbs. Visit places that are far enough from the city to have brokers who handle estates or farm sales. These people frequently inspect properties to evaluate their worth on the market and they may spot an old automobile once in a while. Explain the purpose of your visit and leave a business card or a self-addressed postcard. Finder's fees are usually paid for information that leads to the actual purchase of a car. Be sure

7

This Hupp Skylark had some rust-out in the body but otherwise was in good condition. For this model, Hupp used body dies bought from the defunct Cord company in 1938.

Minor dents and the need for replating are obvious in a close-up view of this Skylark. During the past ten years, models in similar condition have been offered at prices ranging from $300 to $1,200.

to stipulate the latter detail or you may be deluged with the locations of four-teen rusting hulks of flivvers and be billed for each one. Fees noted in ads range from $25 to $100, depending, of course, on the scarcity of the automobile sought. Other possible sources in the country are people who know "everyone and everything" in the area, such as the local postmaster. A half dozen self-addressed postcards left with him may bear fruit. Men who work on farms, like roofers and well diggers, are another source of leads. Long established rural garages are also a potential source of information on "old-timers" in the area. Even if no leads are obtained, you may come across a garage owner who can be coaxed into unearthing old motor manuals and parting with them for a nominal sum.

Attending auction sales at country estates is worthwhile when old auto-mobiles are included in the listing. As knowledgeable as auction people are on almost everything, all of them may not consider old cars to be particularly valuable. A veritable fleet of cars, including Bentleys, Duesenbergs, an Invicta and a Bugatti that had rested neglected in an estate garage, was recently auc-tioned off on Long Island. Despite a large turnout and heavy bidding, most of the cars went for less than their market value.

One area for finding cars of the twenties and thirties has been overlooked to a great extent. This is the upper-middle-class suburbs that were fashionable three or four decades ago when the well-to-do had big houses and two- or three-car garages. Some of these homes are still occupied by the original family, and the likelihood of an old car remaining on the premises is always greater when it is out of the way in a large garage. A few years ago I saw a motorcar pur-chased from such a home when a widow was selling her possessions. It was a 1932 Packard Super Eight touring sedan. The plates on it were from 1938, and that garage must have been dry and snug because even the top was perfectly preserved.

Auto wrecking yards, once a great source, are not as promising today be-cause of their rapid turnover, but nevertheless are not to be ignored. Investi-gate used car lots for possibilities. Although most cars of value found here are in the post-war special interest category, occasional rarities come along. As recently as 1956 I saw a 1903 curved-dash Olds in a Long Island used car lot, sporting what the dealer thought was a fair price of $500. An extremely rare Hupp Skylark was displayed on the busiest highway in Queens County, New York, and remained unsold for months. This is proof that the most obvious place to find a used car, a used car lot, comes through with a real surprise now and then.

THE FUN OF OLD CARS

A relatively new source for antique and classic cars is the dealer specializing in this field. On the East Coast two well-known establishments are the Vintage Car Store of Nyack, New York, and Autos of the Roaring Twenties at Toms River, New Jersey. There are others on the West Coast and elsewhere. These firms offer unrestored cars as well as specimens fit for a museum. A letter will usually bring a list of their latest selections.

Most large towns and the suburban areas of big cities have one or more flourishing all-classified advertising papers. These are a popular means of disposing of older cars with limited trade-in value. A current issue of a Long Island suburban classified weekly contains ads of several late Model Ts, a 1915 Speedster T, a 1929 Packard sedan, a 1931 Auburn and a 1936 Cord Westchester sedan. Prices vary from the ridiculously low to the top current market value, suggesting that some sellers do more research than others. You should also consider the Sunday section of *The New York Times*. Automobiles located

Uncovering a classic. A large horse barn stabled this 1939 Model 327 BMW roadster for many years. The owner of the car brought it home after World War II.

This BMW, being pushed out for examination (*above*) has fine lines and the body appears to be in sound condition. The major work required is a complete engine overhaul.

all over the country are listed in its antique and classic car section. This some-times runs to five half columns, advertising over a hundred cars. Because of its wide readership, *The Times* is also a good place to advertise for a specific car.

The national magazines devoted to cars such as *Road and Track, Car Life* and *Motor Trend* have classified sections where you might find a car of inter-est in your region. Probably the best source for finding the greatest variety of automobiles and parts are the trade papers devoted to the hobby. These may be weekly newsletters or monthly journals. Scanning their classified columns is like attending a flea market of cars and parts. *Hemmings Motor News, The Atlantic Auto Advertiser, Cars and Parts* are a few of the established journals.

Consider advertising for an old car in places other than hobby publications—the bulletin board of the local factory, for example, or in local club bulletins. These long shot efforts may pay off, but in general, the "known" cars for sale will be found where old car fans congregate and will be advertised in the peri-odicals that these people read.

For your initial automobile project no great difficulty should be encountered in finding a suitable car if you are willing to be flexible. If you insist on a Stanley Steamer or a Mercer Raceabout, you will be compounding the diffi-culties of your search for the automobile as well as for its parts. For this rea-son, veteran restorers will often recommend a Model T Ford as an excellent "first" for the novice. The reasons are good. The car is as simple as a car can be (except for the transmission), and an entire industry supplies a mountain of parts for this model. Fifteen million "T"s were made between 1908 and 1927 and for a few hundred dollars you can buy a "Tin Lizzie" in sound condition. Not every fan likes the idea, however, that after several hundred hours of toil his vehicle will be almost indistinguishable from twenty other Model Ts at his first meet.

As you might imagine, most of the choice areas have been gone over with a fine-toothed comb. Twenty years of growing interest in the hobby, coupled with the scrap drives of World War II, have depleted the supply of untouched finds. When you consider that well over three thousand makes of automobiles were produced in America since the turn of the century, however, you may be encouraged to look just a bit further. Surely, rare cars will continue to turn up in the years ahead, even if in diminishing numbers.

Arrivals at an antique car meet.

2. PITFALLS FOR THE UNWARY

SCARCELY any restorer will look back on the first automobile he reclaimed from the ravages of time without the wish that he had done some things differently. There are minor and major mistakes to avoid, of course, some of which only another expert on your car could spot, but the biggest pitfall is the choice of the car itself.

If you are prompted to search for a certain car because of a nostalgic memory of your childhood or college days, no talk of market value will sway you. If the 1927 Hudson Super Six that Uncle Walt drove when he took you fishing in that great summer at Lake George haunts your dreams, finding one and restoring it will probably give you satisfaction. Without this kind of motive or if you're not the lucky fellow who is offered an interesting relic from Grandpa's barn for free, you should keep one key thought in mind: Although this first car will keep you busy now, at some time in the future you may come across another fine car that you would like to acquire and restore. You should acquaint yourself thoroughly with the current market value and degree of desirability your first car will have after restoration. Find this out before investing your time, energy and money on the first old car you consider. This applies to cars in all three categories: antique, classic and special interest. Although the hobby is expanding mightily and values are climbing, it is by no means a safe assumption that any old car will increase in price automatically. Great classic cars in mint restoration are commanding much higher prices today than five, ten or fifteen years ago, not only because of the increased demand, but because of the greatly increased cost of the materials and professional restoration services that have gone into them. Five or six years ago a restored 1937 Cord 812 phaeton might have cost between $4,000 and $6,000. Today prices in excess of $10,000 have been noted. One reason is a trend to a

14

greater degree of authenticity in restoration in that search for "points" at car meets. Another reason is the higher cost of the rare hand skills that few hobbyists possess. At this writing, for example, the current cost in the New York area for a new 812 phaeton interior, that is, leather upholstery, side panels, top and rugs, runs between $1,500 and $2,000. This again points up the desirability of obtaining a car with a sound body and interior. If I had to make a choice between a complete and clean-appearing Cord with mechanical problems and a gutted model with an engine and drive train that had been restored, I would take the former car. I am sure some Cord owners would disagree, but on most cars the hours and materials needed for massive body and interior work usually result in far higher expense than for the average amount of engine work required.

What then should you expect to realize from the sale of a desirable car a year or two after you have restored it? It appears that if you wish to make a profit on your investment in materials, you may well do so. If you include the hundreds and perhaps thousands of hours of labor and expect a commensurate cash return for this, you will be disappointed. Only if the car is one of the really rare, most sought-after classics—a Duesenberg, a Packard Dietrich phaeton or an antique like a Mercer Raceabout—will you be likely to make a substantial overall profit.

A good example of a typical sale was that of a rare European automobile on which the restorer had put in about a year of free time. His investment in the car, including a substantial purchase price, new tires, a huge upholstery bill and a complete mechanical overhaul totaled slightly over $4,000. The automobile was beautifully restored, won a first in its category at Hershey, and attracted several admirers. It was sold for $6,000 and with wider advertising might have brought more. This is considered a sound transaction for both the seller and the buyer. The seller is enabled to go on with his next project and the buyer has purchased a unique car sure to increase in value.

The point to remember is that the cost of restoring a 1929 Graham-Paige or a 1931 Buick sedan may be substantially the same as restoring a 1933 Packard touring sedan or closed coupe. The first two are good cars but undistinguished by almost any definition of fine car or classic car interest. Either Packard, however, is an accepted classic, one being appreciated more for its open body than the other, but both are bound to continue to be sought after by ever-larger numbers of hobbyists. Each of these cars will justify the outlay for the stone guards, running board spotlights, fitted luggage and the myriad of other touches necessary to produce an impressive restoration.

15

THE FUN OF OLD CARS

The 1928 Marmon sedan illustrated here might be used as an example of a car that is credited with full classic status and yet has limited appeal due to its prosaic body style and the degree of restoration required.

This automobile was offered for sale at less than $500, with considerable work already completed. The straight eight engine had been overhauled and was in smooth running order and the body had received a primer coat of paint. The roof had been stripped off some time earlier, and snow and rain had combined to render a worn interior totally unfit. The driver's door will show that although the hardware is intact, new panels, upholstery and small part replating are required. Among the plus factors are a complete instrument panel, unbroken glass and a rust-free body. Minor straightening is required on the bumper irons as well as replating of bumpers and hub caps. The major cost in

Six-window Marmon sedan shows little difference in styling from Grahams or Buicks of the period.

The previous owner concentrated on overhauling the big straight eight Marmon engine.

Sound metal and complete hardware make it possible for the owner to restore this door easily.

The Marmon's instrument panel is virtually complete.

Front view of the Marmon, showing work needed on bumper irons.

If no rot is found, the wooden cross members can support a new roof.

Although the Marmon interior is a shambles, there is enough left of the upholstery and of the arm-rest fixtures to serve as models for exact reproductions.

completing this restoration lies in the stripped roof and gutted interior. Ivan's Auto Upholstery of Farmingdale, New York, a shop that has restored interiors of antique and special interest autos, produced some round-figure estimates for work on this Marmon. (These figures would vary elsewhere, of course, and are intended merely as a guide.) A new roof of authentic materials and a new head liner would be around $200. Restoring the door panels and complete re-upholstery of the interior in cloth would add $300 or $400. Carpets of deep pile would run another $100. These were approximations and the final total might be near $1,000. Add to this the cost of a quality lacquer paint job, which can be from $200 to $400, and a new set of classic whitewalls, 650 x 19 six-ply tires at $60 each, and the grand total might range from $1,800 to $2,000 for buying and restoring this Marmon.

It is strongly recommended that the expense required for restoring a car of marginal appeal be investigated. A recent advertisement in a hobby publication listed a 1930 Marmon sedan in mint condition at $1,200. Does this mean that for economic reasons such a classic as the unrestored 1928 Marmon must be consigned to the junk yard? Not at all; much of the cost of restoration could be reduced if the owner acquires the proficiency to perform some of the skilled jobs. Jackson Bailey, active in Lincoln Continental restoration, has said that one of the finest paint jobs he had ever seen had been done by a car owner with a $40 mail-order spray unit. If the seat upholstery on the Marmon is for a specialist, how about the roof? Reprints of step-by-step instructions for replacing a roof are available and this skill can be mastered. The header could be left to the specialist for a perfect fit. The hobby advertisements frequently list used sets of tires with 50 per cent or more of tread at about a third the cost of new rubber. Scraping and varnishing the wooden wheels is a simple, if tedious, job for the owner to do. Carpet cost could be cut to $20 by using foam-backed rugs cut to fit stencils carefully made of brown paper. Rubber-backed carpeting does not have to be bound. Even including rental of a paint sprayer and the raw materials for the roof exterior, and still retaining the benefit of professional work on the head liner, seat upholstery and door panels, overall cost could be cut in half.

When the purchase of a car is contemplated, make a list of the things to be done for restoration. A quick check with fellow club members might reveal that you have skilled help available for those areas in which you are weak. If the car is missing tires or wire wheels or headlamps, a scanning of back issues of journals like *Hemmings Motor News* should give you an idea of the cost when you do find the needed part. A pair of three-bulb Marchal headlamps for a vintage Bentley might run as high as $150, while a pair of fine Graham-Paige headlights complete with crossbar would be $15.

Remember, much of the body structure of cars built before the middle thirties is wood, sheathed in steel or aluminum panels. The metal on door panels and body sills can appear sound and yet hide a structure weakened by dry rot. The most obvious way to spot this is to examine the hinge and lock pillars on all door frames. Use some force and see if the partly open door can be pushed up or down appreciably. Rotted wood won't be able to withstand this kind of pressure and the hinge will move noticeably. Find the body bolts connecting the body to the frame and try to move them. Use a prying motion with a pinch bar or large screwdriver. Gently does it! No body bolt movement is a fair sign the wood is sound.

A point often forgotten is glass. Just because it's all there and no cracks are evident doesn't mean it is satisfactory. Remember, a classic car must have safety glass to compete in meets, not to mention for the protection the owner will want his family to have. Early cars may have a safety glass windshield and plate glass elsewhere. To remove and replace all glass on a sedan can add up to a substantial amount. Use the coin or match reflection test if no manufacturer's label is found. Twin reflections indicate plate glass that will have to go, four reflections (caused by laminations) indicate safety glass. Some few automobiles had mesh or parallel wires in plate glass in the early days of experimentation, and such cars would have to be approved or rejected individually. Don't forget to check wind-wing glass as well. If this is plate, be sure to make an accurate tracing for the safety glass replacement.

Although not a great deal can be determined by looking at the outside of a dirt-encrusted engine, a few steps are essential. Don't accept the premise that everything is there without checking. It has happened before that a restoration novice has towed home a prize to find out later that the crankcase housing and the crankshaft were missing. Turn the crank handle; just determining if the engine is free is an essential first step. If the car is a rare model, it is of great importance that engine accessories be present. If pump, carburetor or magneto are unrestorable, you will at least have the nomenclature to start hunting for replacements.

A spray can of engine cleaner is handy to have along. A quick cleaning will reveal serious cracks in the crankcase, transmission, or any other housing that would be expensive to replace.

If you can bring any literature when first viewing the car, you may find the model year claimed is incorrect. On looking at Model T Fords, some of the

20

Floyd Clymer publications that illustrate every model would be a valuable aid. These cars frequently have updated or mismatched fenders and this is a tedious item to correct.

If the tires are "checked" badly, they will need replacing. They may be holding air because the owner pumped them up an hour before your arrival. Tires on which the car's weight has not rested are often quite good, but regardless of appearances, few hobbyists wish to rely on a tire casing that has been drying out for twenty or more years. Regardless of the car's mechanical condition, refrain from running at speed on the tires unless a tire expert has approved their condition. A full-page tire advertisement from a hobby publication that itemizes hundreds of sizes can help you to determine exactly what a replacement set will cost.

If the investment is large and many questions arise on the car you are considering, you may be wise to offer a small binder to the owner. If you can obtain several days or a week to locate, through your regional club membership, a fellow enthusiast who is an expert on this make, you may avoid a real problem car.

After having weighed the merits of the car and having decided to buy it for your maiden project, a word of advice on bringing it home. Unless it has been registered and run quite recently, within a year or two, don't consider driving it. The chance of doing considerable damage to the engine or of having an accident because of unfamiliarity with the automobile makes this unwise. If at all possible, bring it home on a trailer. If one cannot be borrowed or hired, the car can either be towed home or loaded into a van-type truck.

During your restoration work, hew to the straight and narrow line of authenticity. It will be frustrating at times to be held up for the lack of some minor part or accessory. When you're tempted to put those parking lights from a Studebaker President on your Packard because they look "pretty close," go out for a round of golf instead. Almost anything missing can be found today if all the hobby publications are consulted diligently enough and long enough. When you ease your restored automobile into the line at an important meet, you will be proud of your detective work in insuring a completely authentic restoration. Authenticity is vital in selling your car, should that time come, and a restored automobile is really only a worthy addition to our genuine Americana when it is entirely authentic.

3. RESTORATION HINTS FOR PUTTING YOUR CAR IN SHAPE

BY the time you have selected a car to restore, you will have decided to a large degree just how much work you will do yourself. The amount of space and the number of tools you need will depend on this factor. Ideally, a garage should be at least fifteen feet in width if you want to remove major parts and work on them conveniently. A two-car garage will allow you to place the chassis on saw horses on one side and the body similarly supported on the other, with plenty of space in between to work in. If this is not possible, you may have to store the body outdoors under a tarp. It may seem unnecessary to state, but be sure you have adequate tackle and headroom before attempting to remove the body in your garage. A local gas station may have to do this for you. The chassis and body can be trailered home separately.

If you plan to do minor mechanical work on your automobile and to complete the restoration with a simple refurbishing of the body, your tool needs will be limited. The normal sets of open-end and box-end wrenches (a metric set if your car is European), a hacksaw, a hand electric drill, a bench belt sander, and the usual chisels, files, etc., found in a homeowner's garage will suffice. A workbench (with a vise) with ample lighting is also essential. A curved jaw locking wrench is valuable for removing frozen bolts. A supply of penetrating oil or Liquid Wrench is a necessity. A regular and a ball peen hammer, and a rawhide hammer should be stocked. This last is an absolute must if your vintage car has knock-off wire wheel hubs. A set of screwdrivers and pliers, including an electrician's type, will be needed.

If you have the skills and the intention of doing all restoration from the frame up, you very likely have the necessary machine tools. If not, consult a fellow club member who has a home shop equipped for a complete restoration procedure. The lathe, drill press, bench grinder, band saw, as well as the weld-

22

ing and paint spraying equipment needed, should be selected with the advice of an expert in their use.

Orderly Procedure: It is wise to label or tag each part as you remove it from the car. The disassembled small units should be sketched quickly in an exploded view and the sketch filed on a convenient clipboard. Many restorers simply lay the parts out in sequence and photograph them in Polaroid for their file. Loose bolts are best kept in their original holes while the removed part is out for sandblasting or plating. Remember that it may take months to locate some parts, so one of the first steps is to make a list of the ones you will need. While you are working on other parts of the vehicle, you can be shopping for those elusive items.

Tires, No Longer a Problem: In the early days of the antique car restoration movement, one of the biggest problems was the location of tires no longer made. When found, they were often so checked or rotted as to be unsafe. Happily, after many years of Firestone holding the fort alone, other firms are issuing a wide range of types and sizes.

One of the widest selections, including Clinchers and Straight Sides, all-whites, and in rim sizes up to 38 inches, is offered by PJA Pneumatic. Other makers include Denman (especially in the classic sizes), Goodyear, Firestone, Dunlop, General, Vogue, and there are several mail-order-house brands. Firestone even makes several kinds of solid tires used on early trucks. All of these tire makers advertise in hobby publications, and their distributors cover the country.

Costs vary widely, depending on the size and the amount of handwork on a particular tire and the size of the market for that tire. The 3.50 x 30, commonly

The tire is worthless, but the chassis and running gear of this Buick are sound.

This side lamp, made in Berlin for the 1914 Benz, is a challenge to the restorer's skill. The broken side lens is bevel-cut in one piece with the darker section dyed blue.

used on Model Ts, ranges from $30 to $45 plus the tube. A 475./5.00 x 19 may run as low as $18. A 700 x 21 six-ply in white would be about $100 each.

Those Brass Lamps: It is rare to acquire an antique car of pre-World War I days with its brass lamps intact. Frequently all five—head lamps, side lamps and tail lamp—will be missing. Your first step will be to determine authentic units for your automobile. During the days of assembled cars, many builders furnished several different makes of lamps on their vehicles, which will simplify your search. They may have been Rushmore, Deitz or 20th Century brass lamps, among others. For some reason, perhaps Yankee thrift, when many old cars were junked the lamps would be stuck away in the attic or barn. They have been avidly sought out, and scores of them are listed in hobby publications. Original matched head lamps in fine condition command good prices, from $75 to $150. If you have units that have bent sections or cracked lenses, don't despair, they can usually be rebuilt like new. If lenses are mostly complete but broken into several pieces, a mold can be made and a plastic substitute cast to serve until an original glass lens is found. If parts of the brass case are damaged beyond repair but are of a round shape, new parts can be spun in yellow brass to match. Sections with octagonal-shaped rims, however, must be hammered out to shape, a difficult procedure.

Thorough research on a brass-age restoration will pay off. Combing old car advertisements from the *Century Magazine, Harper's,* and *The Horseless Age* will frequently provide you with a picture and nomenclature of head lamps, side lamps, horns and other accessories for your car.

If your brass lamps or horn have age cracks that are not wide, they may be filled with silver solder. The edges should be smoothed first. After the crack has been filled, using a small torch, level the surface with emery cloth and buff.

The endless and frequent polishing brass requires can be kept to a minimum by fashioning a plastic cover for each fixture.

A final word on the lighting ability of early acetylene gas lamps for modern driving: Most hobbyists rarely drive their brass-age cars after dark—in fact it is forbidden in many states by motor vehicle law unless supplementary lights are used. For these lights you can clamp on sealed beam units with a temporary wiring harness. At the next meet you attend see how other early car owners have rigged these temporary light units.

Fenders: Fix or Find? Up to ten or fifteen years ago there seemed to be more necessity to repair fenders and other rusted-out or damaged sheet metal in a car under restoration. With the exception of Fords, it was the prospect of a long fruitless search for a sound replacement part that compelled the restorer to make do with what he had. Ironically, the number of "parts cars" was higher, but the means of locating them were limited. The basic procedure, then as now, when a rare fender or door could not be replaced, was the insertion of new sheet metal in the rotted area. For the hobbyist who has mastered welding, this is not complicated. The damaged part is removed from the car, and placed on a suitable bench. It should be thoroughly cleaned so that the entire rusted-through area is known, then a brown paper pattern made. The paper should be taped to a perfect fit over the fender curve and accurate marks made on both the fender and the pattern to insure an exact fit for the piece going in. Making sure the gauge is the same, cut new sheet metal to fit, weld in place and then grind down the seams smoothly. Simple curves and large flat areas are safest for the novice to perfect his technique. A large Packard front fender with a rusted-out bottom in the wheel well might be attempted because if less than flawless, it won't show. A new hood, particularly with cut louvers, should be left to the experts, as nothing is more noticeable on a car than a poorly fitted hood.

Today, with the wealth of club bulletins and hobby journals, the restorer

The owner, Charles Hartman, runs wiring through to the headlights of the 1914 Benz.

Joseph Thamm applies a final coat to the Benz fender. Newspapers protect the mahogany body.

This rare tool can be adjusted to put various shapes of rolled edges on the flat uncrowned fenders used on very early automobiles.

can often simplify the whole fender problem by finding a sound replacement. It is hard to be specific, but the cost will usually range from $10 to $30, plus shipping charges, for a solid specimen for the typical Model T. Fenders for special-interest cars of the early thirties are generally in the same price range. Those for the big classics, particularly wheel well fenders, command somewhat higher prices. It is surprising how often "new old stock" turns up, that is, fenders that have never been on a car and are literally new.

Into the Engine: How far one goes in a restoration project is a subject that

A Long Island Lincoln Continental enthusiast has acquired a small fleet of 1940 to 1948 "parts cars" and has been able to furnish many needed replacements to other restorers.

An engine compartment of a Buick in "as-found condition." The newcomer will soon develop an "eye" for seeing through dirt and rust to judge the basic condition of a car.

is hotly debated. Some wealthy collectors will buy a car that has been restored, send it into a shop, and have it torn down to the engine block and frame. It will then be re-restored at great expense, because one person's definition of the word differs sharply from another's.

A basket case, or a car with major parts missing, will of necessity be restored from the ground up and the end result will, hopefully, duplicate the vehicle's appearance and its internal tolerances when new. Owners differ over the degree of restoration needed for cars that are mechanically sound when bought. One man will take down a purring Hisso engine and do a complete overhaul, while another will perhaps only do a valve job. Each owner makes his own decision, depending on his degree of satisfaction with the mechanical condition of his car.

When appraising a car for purchase, by all means count on the most pessimistic estimate for restoration if the engine is an unknown factor. Anticipate the cost of a rebore, rings, pistons, new bearings, valve springs, ring guides, and the like. If you have acquired a smooth-running Pierce or Packard, however, with a low-stressed, low-mileage engine that checks out well, think twice before doing unnecessary work. Several of the fine automobiles illustrated here required very little work on their engines.

The technical aspects of restoration have been well covered in several books. The experienced mechanic already knows the value of the appropriate Dykes manual for his vintage car. Every month more reprints of early shop manuals become available and are of great value, even for an expert, when working on

27

an unfamiliar engine. Comb the hobby periodicals to see if a manual for your car is obtainable, either an original or reprint.

Bright Work—Some Replating Tips: Virtually every old car will require some replating. Before a major part is sent out, the original plating should be positively identified. Some early classics, such as the Hispano-Suiza, the Rolls-Royce and the Isotta-Fraschini, as well as some American cars like the Peerless, had radiator shells of German or nickel silver. The gleaming appearance of this metal can frequently be restored by jeweler's rouge and a buffing. It is accepted practice today to replate nickeled parts with chrome for better appearance and easier maintenance. In a showdown between otherwise equal cars at a Model A meet, however, the car with the original nickel plating will earn a few more points.

It is essential that you shop carefully for your plating work. If fellow club members have had good results from a particular source, benefit from their experience. Remember, all the replating firm is contracting for is the new surface. If you deliver a headlight shell with minor dents left in it, it will be replated as delivered. On castings it is important to file off pitting irregularities and fill minor holes for a smooth surface. Before deciding that a particular part must be replated, consider the possibility of replacing it with a part in

The Hooper aluminum body of this 1934 Rolls-Royce presented a problem when the removal of paint revealed poorly mended body damage. As the thin metal sheets could burn away in the welding process, Epoxy resin putty and Fiberglas were used instead. The patched area, which was later sanded down, is as strong as metal.

Detail of patched area before sanding.

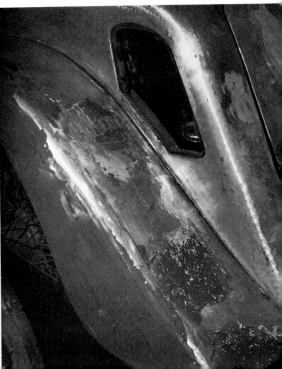

better condition. A 1942 Lincoln Continental I inspected recently had a pitted grill. Replating all six sections, after considerable preparatory work by the owner, would average $25 per unit, or about $150. About the same time I had noted a hobby ad for a factory-fresh 1942 grill, absolutely mint, offered at $95. In this case it would seem logical for the restorer to snap this up and advertise the pitted grill for a nominal sum. Good chrome work should last five to ten years and is essential to a fine restoration.

Leather or Plastic? Despite the difference in cost, and it is almost double, there seems to be a trend for upholstering a fine open classic car with genuine leather when that was the original material. Several of the modern plastics are long-wearing and practical, but their early popularity is declining in the drive for authenticity. Are there any ways to beat the high cost of an all-new custom leather installation? Leather is an amazingly durable material; though scuffed and abused, it can sometimes be removed, treated, dyed and replaced at a fraction of the cost of new leather. New flexible paints, which can be applied right on the cushions, will not crack or craze or affect the suppleness of the leather. If an interior is sound except for one or two torn sections, it is possible to cut out the damaged rolled and pleated section and replace it with a matching section of new leather. *The Restoration of Antique and Classic Cars* by Richard Wheatley and Brian Morgan gives graphic instructions for this procedure. Cars that were originally furnished with leatherette interiors should not be glamorized with genuine leather.

Woodwork: Wheels to Dashboard. Woodwork on old cars can be both visible and invisible. On an early tourer, wooden trim on door tops and the instrument panel will test your skill at refinishing. Frequently the wooden frame of the metal-covered body will require work. Here it is a question of restoring structural strength and the new sheet metal will cover the work on the frame. The replacement of the dash is the most common piece of woodwork needed on early cars. This is usually simple because only one or two flat pieces are involved. Use the original dash as a pattern for all screw holes and instrument cut-outs. Determine the kind of wood used in the original. A marine-grade plywood of the same grain and color is often obtainable. Replacing wooden bows should usually be done by a specialist if you are unable to find a set you can refinish.

Wooden wheels are easily refinished. Before the tedious scraping down to bare wood, best accomplished by using a broken piece of bottle glass as a tool, check every spoke and the felloes for rot. Slight looseness of a spoke can sometimes be remedied with Epoxy resin glue. Should replacements of spokes be needed, it is advisable to send the wheel to a reputable wheelwright.

(*Far left*) This Marmon wheel is typical of the popular artillery type once universally used. Wood rot is the major source of trouble in these durable wheels.

(*Left*) Broken glass is the best tool for scraping wooden spokes. If several coats of paint are present chemical removers may be necessary.

Parts That Can't Be Found. Occasionally the restorer will run into a blank wall when searching for one or more vital parts. It is possible to mend and patch sheet metal, as a visit to any modern fender and body shop will indicate, but what can be done when the missing part is a casting? The 1912 Case illustrated here was found with but one original Case wheel hub, a large brass casting with the maker's name in relief. Owner Charles Hartman took this one hub to a reliable foundry and ordered unfinished duplicates. The procedure followed is to coat the original part with beeswax to a depth of about $\frac{1}{16}$ of an inch. A sand mold is then made and duplicates cast in brass. The beeswax is to allow for shrinkage in cooling. The rough casting was finished by Mr. Hartman on his lathe and by hand filing and polishing to the original hub dimensions. To insure an accurate fit of the threaded hub, a steel mandril was threaded to fit the original Case part and a constant check made as the new hubs were cut for threads. Foundry charges were based on the weight of the brass and to insure against possible future loss or theft, Mr. Hartman ordered several extra. It is virtually impossible to detect the reproductions from the original.

Model T and Model A—the Smoothest Path. It is a truism of business that the biggest market will be served best. In the old car field this is demonstrated by the virtual supermarket of parts and services available for the owners of ancient Fords. It is estimated that 300,000 of the close to 5,000,000 Model As made are still running. Triple that amount of Tin Lizzies were made and a proportionate number of them survive. There are more "T"s and "A"s being restored than any other automobiles and probably more than all the classics combined. In the past ten years a huge business has come into being, supplying the needs of Ford owners. At first the firms sold only original old stock and used parts, but now they have gone into the large-scale manufacture of reproduction parts. For the Model T owner this means he can obtain all new sheet metal, such as fenders, running board shields, hoods, seat frames, trunk lids and whole body sides. He can find new hub caps, script, wooden coil boxes, brass step plates, windshield frames, motor meters and even the exact patent plate for his model car. Under the hood virtually every item needed for a factory-new rebuild on the Model T engine is available.

The Model A restorer is at least as well catered to. Should he have a coupe or sedan with a rotted-out or missing roof, he may purchase a complete kit containing the authentic Cobra Grain Decking, the padding, caulking, welting and all hardware. Depending on the model, these kits cost between $10 and $25, a far cry from the cost of such work done in a body shop. Body sheet metal sections for "A"s and even complete upholstered rumble seats are available. Complete pre-cut and finished upholstery kits are made for both "T"s and "A"s. Model T owners can convert their cars by installing a complete wooden reproduction speedster or Depot Hack body on their chassis for $200 to $400. Running boards or wind wings, instruments or top bows, all are available. The purist will search for original parts when possible, but most reproductions are satisfactory substitutes. As stated before, if the newcomer to the automobile restoration hobby has no strong preference for a particular car, the choice of a Ford for the maiden project is recommended. They abound, and the market value seems easier to determine for these cars than for many others. A Model T of the twenties can be bought today in restorable condition at a price ranging from $200 to $600. In mint condition it may command from $1,200 to $2,500. Model A owners have found values soaring for well-restored cars. This car demands a fanatical attention to authenticity in every respect if the owner hopes to triumph at meets. Both Ford models are small and compact, allowing the restorer to make do with a one-car garage workshop, both are inexpensive to register and run, and both are readily saleable.

Experimentation in new restoration techniques and materials for all cars is constantly going on. The logical clearing house for this information is the clubs. Their various publications often feature pages of tips sent in by members. Attendance at your local meetings and meets will pay practical dividends when you discover how other hobbyists have solved their restoration problems.

Rough hub castings, returned by the foundry, have been duplicated from the one original Case hub.

4. THE ANTIQUE AUTOMOBILE

JUST about any automobile whose roof looms a foot or two higher than today's family car will produce the exclamation, "There goes an antique car!" Actually, the term antique applied to cars is frequently nebulous, misleading and confusing. Many classic cars are also antiques and so are some special-interest automobiles. In obtaining plates for an old car, it is important to consult your state's motor vehicle regulations and see what is considered "antique." Most states classify an automobile as antique if it is twenty-five to forty years old. Some states issue a permanent plate, others have a low-cost annual fee for antique cars. Many issue special plates inscribed Ancient Car, Old Car or Historical Car.

The basic authorities for classification of a vehicle, from a collector's viewpoint, are, of course, the clubs. Three national clubs are primarily concerned with the antique category. They include the two oldest: The Antique Automobile Club of America, founded in 1935 and The Horseless Carriage Club of America, established in 1937. The third major club is The Veteran Motor Car Club of America.

This last-mentioned club uses the figure of thirty-five years as a criterion of veteran or antique status. Each passing year allows another production year of automobiles to qualify. The Antique Automobile Club of America considers that all pre-1930 models qualify as antique. The Horseless Carriage Club, being more interested in the early examples of motor cars, limits their choice for antique designation to cars produced before 1916.

To encourage interest in all old cars, virtually all the clubs make provisions for attendance at meets of cars other than their specialties. The hard-and-fast rules concern enrollment of a car for judging, awards, and official status in a particular club.

33

(*Opposite*) The Rolls-Royce Silver Ghost

The true fascination of restoring and driving old cars started with antiques. Their appeal lies, in great part, in their link with a radically different age— the age when the electric light was unknown or rare, the airplane a novelty to gape at in the south meadow when a barnstormer came along on a hot summer day, and the pace of life was the pace behind a team of horses. Modern science has yet to create the time machine of H. G. Wells, but we have such machines in abundance. Climb into the Edwardian parlor interior of a 1912 Case, for example, on a warm summer night. When the acetylene lamps are lit and the engine cranked over to a steady hum, run out to a country road off the parkway where the air smells of farmland and you are transported to a tranquil bygone age.

1900 LOCOMOBILE, STYLE 2

WE LOOK back to steam automobiles as an expression of the exotic and daring in early car design, yet to many automobile makers around the turn of the century, steam was the logical, conservative choice. It was then the oldest and the proven power. It had driven locomotives and threshers for decades, it ran stationary engines, ships, sawmills, and had even been tried in an early aircraft and a motorcycle. The steamer was invented and developed in America by F. E. and F. O. Stanley, twin brothers. In 1916, they advertised their engine as proven "a hundred years," referring to Stephenson's design for a steam engine.

The lever in the floorboard is the control for an auxiliary hand-feed water pump.

In their early years, Locomobile developed a world-wide sales force. This steamer, headed for Hobart Town in Tasmania, is a long way from the plant at Bridgeport, Connecticut.

The virtues of the Stanley Steamer were its quiet, vibrationless ride and its smooth flow of power, a noisy gear box being unnecessary. Power for hill climbing and exceptional speed on the level were also characteristics of the steamers. Among their disadvantages were the time necessary to get up steam and the limited range because of the need for frequent replenishment of the water supply. Eventually these problems were solved, but too late to overcome the lead taken by the gas engine. No doubt, dire murmurings from rival car salesmen about the foolhardiness of riding about "on top of a fire" above a boiler that could blow the driver to kingdom come didn't help the steamer's image. No matter that no recorded instance could be found to illustrate a boiler explosion, the public was ready to believe that such stories could be suppressed. Tests indicated that Stanley boilers could withstand four times the pressure of 600 pounds per square inch they operated under.

The Locomobile pictured here was made early in the company's production, the Locomobile Company having bought out the Stanleys in 1899. A complicated seesaw of legal skirmishes was waged over the next several years. The Stanley brothers had contracted to refrain from making steam vehicles for a

36

five-year period, but they resumed production in 1902. They contended their new designs differed substantially from the early steamers. In any event, Locomobile prospered, delivering 5,000 machines by 1903.

According to the ads of the day, the car was virtually foolproof, but an owner in England expressed some other thoughts in a letter thus:

> I suppose she will settle down some day to her conception of duty but just now her record is one of eternal and continuous breakdown. She disgraced us on June 26th when I took two friends over thirteen miles of flat road. The pumps failed to lift and we had to pump dolefully every few miles home. Also she took to blowing out her pistons. . . . On June 30th I telephoned up to town and got the London agents to send a man down to overhaul. She needed repacking throughout, and the main steam valve leaked. . . . She covered the five miles from the station to my home in fine form. Yesterday, July 3rd, I went out for an evening trip—a few miles only along the

The front steering arm in the picture was missing and the owner, borrowing the part from another restored Locomobile, machined an exact duplicate.

Note the steering knuckle of the steel bicycle-type wheel. The tires are 2½ x 28 inches. The original tires were white rubber, but black rubber is an acceptable substitute.

Controls at the side-tiller driver's position. The long lever inside the railing is the throttle, while the shorter one outside is the forward and reverse control. At the base of this lever is a by-pass valve to restore excess water to the tank.

road. Her steam was beautiful, but she shut down her fire automatically, and amid the jeers of Brighton we crawled to the repair shop where we left her. The explanation was that her petrol pipe was plugged. . . . It is true that she is noiseless but so is a corpse and one does not get much fun out of a corpse!

The writer signed himself "Locomobiliously, Rudyard Kipling."

Perhaps the ocean voyage from Bridgeport to Sussex didn't agree with the famed writer's machine, because dependability was becoming a byword with Locomobiles by this time.

Edward Berry obtained his Locomobile, incomplete and in the condition referred to as a basket case, from a collection of unrestored machines owned by Austin Clark, the noted authority on antique and classic cars. It had been in the possession of the Stevens Institute for some years but its condition apparently discouraged all who had considered buying it. Mr. Berry was encouraged to find the running gear virtually complete, the two-cylinder steam engine in good condition, and the hopeless body sufficiently intact to provide correct patterns for restoration. The bicycle-type wheels needed respoking, and the pumps and the vital boiler were missing. Failing to locate a boiler, Mr. Berry tackled the job himself and built an exact duplicate, a job for which a local boiler works had quoted a price of $700. Certain linkage including the steering arm was missing and Mr. Berry borrowed the part from another Locomobile owner and made an exact duplicate. At a flea market in Hershey, Pennsylvania, he spotted a brand-new set of rear-end gears and acquired them for spares. The Solar lamps appear on the machine in a 1900 advertisement and that was sufficient to authenticate them. Of the original equipment supplied with this two-seater, Mr. Berry lacks only the tool set, the Bermuda gong and the rubber folding bucket.

This model originally sold for $750 f.o.b. Bridgeport, Connecticut. Its wheelbase is 58 inches and tread 54 inches. It carries five gallons of fuel (kerosene) and twenty-six gallons of water. Tires are 2½ x 28 inch pneumatics mounted on steel wheels. The engine is a double-action two-cylinder 2½ x 3½ inch, using superheated steam. Brakes work directly on the exposed differential gear.

Solar side lamps used carbide fuel.

The Locomobile steam engine, barely 2 feet long, featured two double-acting cylinders, 2½ x 3½ inches, using superheated steam.

Detail of rear sprocket. The double-acting brake worked directly on the differential gear.

Spring suspension is traverse style, while the Stanleys favored fore and aft elliptics at the time. Advertised speed was 45 mph, which seems rather hair-raising today for such a spidery vehicle.

Locomobile soon turned to making large, powerful gas-engine cars and produced the highest-quality type of vehicle until the firm's demise in 1929. That year also spelled ruin for another steam pioneer who had carried steam into the modern car age, solving virtually all its inherent problems. That man was Abner Doble, whose California-built E-series Doble Steamer had achieved renown, although few orders. Its starting time via electric ignition was 23 seconds, and 40 mph was attained in 13 seconds. Mr. Doble's company closed in 1931 and so ended the last American production steam passenger car. Doble later joined Henschel of Germany, and the fleets of steam buses and trucks produced under his patents until 1940 proved that steam has a place on today's highways. As recently as 1954 the Paxton Company was experimenting with an advanced prototype steamer, and steam enthusiasts refuse to admit that the smooth and silent power of steam will not someday add its gentle refinement to our noisy parkways.

Traverse springs and steering-knuckle design.

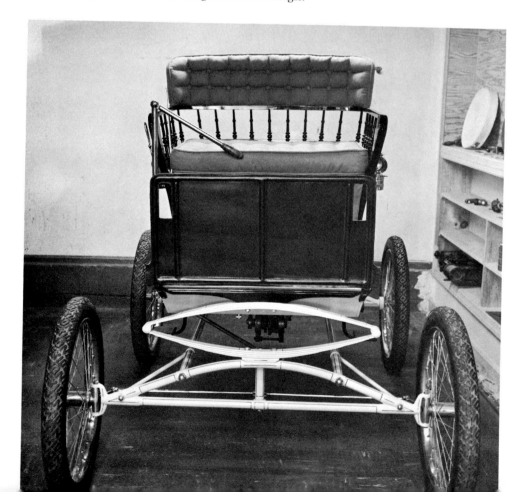

The Sears Auto-Buggy was noted for its ability to negotiate deeply rutted roads as this view of the "high-wheeler" indicates.

1908 SEARS
BUSINESS RUNABOUT,
MODEL J

THE TERM Horseless Carriage fits few vehicles as well as the austere high-wheelers that lingered up to the beginning of World War I. They can be immediately recognized by their solid-tired carriage wheels and buggylike bodies. They enjoyed considerable popularity with farmers and doctors who liked the way the huge wheels could travel deeply rutted country lanes. Most makes had twin-cylinder engines developing less than 15 h.p., more than ample for a vehicle weighing 1,100 or 1,200 pounds. The Sears, which was manufactured from 1906 to 1911 virtually unchanged, scarcely differs in general appearance from the Duryea of 1895. Despite their virtues, these cars always looked old-fashioned, and this helped to finish them when the far-advanced Model T entered the field in 1908.

The Sears Auto Buggy, as it was called, was well made and was a good value for $395 in 1908. The famed mail-order company turned out some 4,000 machines altogether, of which about eighty are preserved today. The most interesting points of this car are its two-cylinder air-cooled engine and the

Left-hand side-tiller steering was a feature of the Sears. Tiny levers near the tiller are spark and throttle controls.

With the floorboard removed, the two-cylinder horizontal-opposed type motor can be seen. It develops 14 h.p. with a bore and stroke of $4\frac{1}{8}$ x 4 inches.

ingenious friction-drive transmission it employed. Other makes of the period, including Metz and Cartercar, used this drive system. One problem was the rapid wear of the friction band that rotated against the huge flywheel. If the driver carelessly engaged the "clutch," wear equivalent to hundreds of miles of driving could occur in an instant. Under ideal conditions a full gas tank could propel the Sears 150 miles at its most comfortable cruising speed, about 18 mph.

Harold Kraft located his Sears Auto Buggy in the early forties on Long Island. It had been stored with other antique automobiles in a barn. When the structure was swept by fire, the Sears was left in sad condition. Its wheels were virtually consumed and its wooden body was usable only as a pattern for a replica which Mr. Kraft built in his cellar over a period of several years. Fortunately, the running gear and all brass were intact and readily restored. A long search and much swapping finally led to the acquisition of four genuine Sears wheels in good condition. Epoxy glue was used to tighten their wobbly spokes. A carriage restorer for a local museum mounted new $1\frac{1}{8}$ x 36 inch solid tires on them. The engine required extensive work, but strangely enough, the twin mufflers are original.

In its day the Sears had appeal for the conservative buyers who would tolerate an automobile if it resembled the carriages they were used to. Even its low price and easy maintenance (and the eventual addition of pneumatic tires) couldn't save it from the onslaught of the Model T, and the highwheelers, after a decade of popularity, faded into automotive history.

One of the two drive chains. A clutch mechanism provided differential action by controlling the speed of each chain separately.

A wheel carrying a friction band revolved against the huge flywheel, hence the term friction drive. When the friction band was made to pass across the center of the flywheel, it reversed the direction of the vehicle.

Spring detail and headlamp of the Auto Buggy.

Rear view shows large sprocket on the drive wheels.

1908 JACKSON TOURING CAR, MODEL H

FOUNDED in its namesake Michigan city in the year the Wrights first flew, 1903, this aggressive automobile firm lasted just twenty years. In the hectic competition of those pre-World War I days, the Jackson Company took on all comers.

Entered in the Sixth Vanderbilt Cup Race in 1910, a 354-cubic-inch Jackson faced giants like the Alco-6, the Simplex, Mercedes and Apperson. These brutes and many of the other thirty-odd entries crowded the 600-cubic-inch limit. It would be nice to say the Jackson won, but although it didn't, driver Schiefler and his machine were still running at the end of the race. Quite an achievement, considering that more than half the contestants cracked up or broke down before the race was ended. Encouraged no doubt by this exhibition of stamina, a Jackson was entered in the Seventh Vanderbilt Cup race the following year, but due to engine failure it lasted just one lap. So ended the Jackson's efforts to place in the most important races of its day.

Front end of the Jackson reveals the attention to detail, such as pin striping the springs and crank handle, that marks a superb restoration.

(*Opposite*) The Jackson still retained the wheel at the right, as did a majority of American cars at this time.

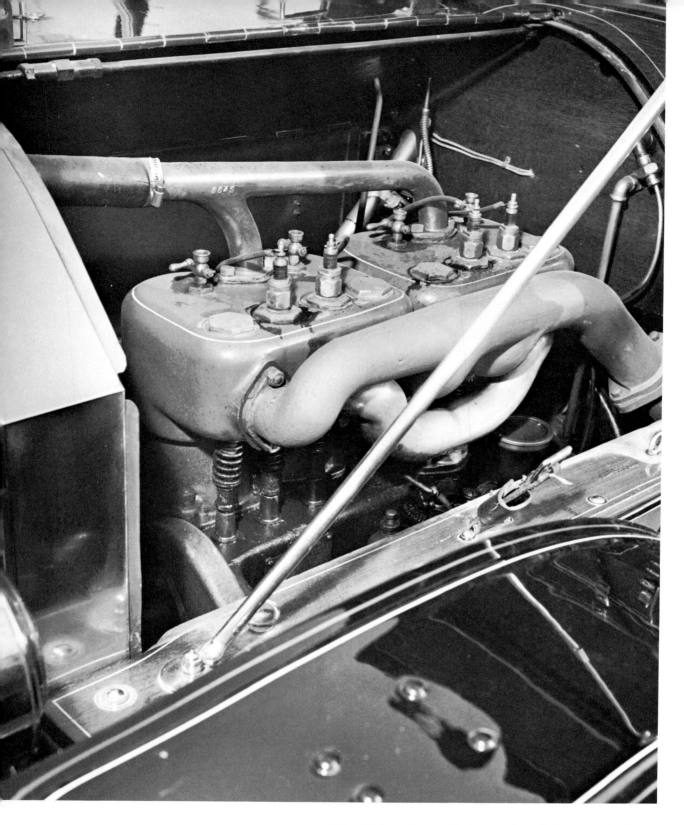

The 30 h.p. four-cylinder engine of the 1908 Jackson.

The Jackson's slogan was cocky and forthright: "No Hill Too Steep, No Sand Too Deep." Judging from the ease with which owner Joseph Thamm's Model H climbs a steep grade near his home, it was no empty boast. When first located in 1947, this Jackson wore the crest of the Socony Oil Company on its door. Although it had seen harder service than a privately owned vehicle, it was quite solid. The original upholstery was almost completely gone, having been devoured by rats which had apparently nested in the exhaust pipe. Tires and tubes were rotted away, but the wheels and rims were sound. The top was in tatters, but all the bows were intact. The dash presented a problem. It was finally removed and used as a template for an exact replacement in marine-grade plywood. The body wood, of ash, was intact. The original brass and fiber spark plugs were good and are still in use. Clutch and brakes are also original. The windshield glass was whole, but Mr. Thamm replaced it with shatter-proof as most clubs recommend, when possible.

Mr. Thamm is currently restoring a Rolls-Royce of a much more recent vintage. He owns a Model T and a 1915 Buick, but the Jackson remains his favorite for meets, touring and fun driving around Long Island. He hasn't tried the "No Sand Too Deep" test, but apparently there is "No Hill Too Steep" for this brass-age tourer.

The restored dash. Note the oil gauge (next to the fire extinguisher) and the ignition box.

Virtually all sliding-gear-change automobiles had adapted the Packard-introduced "H" pattern gear box by this time, and the Jackson was no exception.

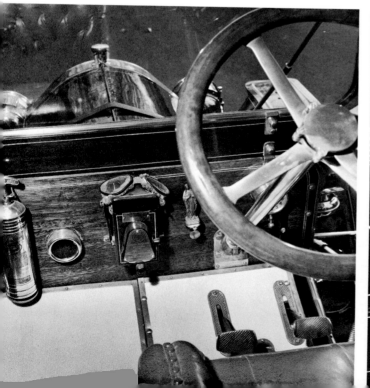

(*Left*) The Jackson incorporated a storage locker under the rear seat. Map pockets were provided in the doors.

(*Below*) Detail shows side lamp, speedometer and elaborate brass horn.

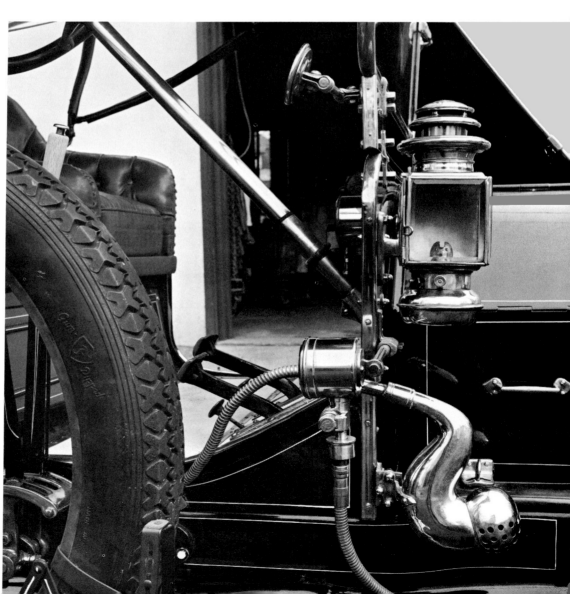

Huge acetylene headlamp of the Jackson. This Neverout Searchlight Projector was widely used on scores of makes at this time.

Profile view shows the true proportions of the car and side-mounted spare.

Finished in the original color scheme of deep blue with yellow striping, the Courier presents a dashing picture.

The Courier Car

(Licensed Under Selden Patent)

1910 COURIER SPEEDSTER
MODEL 10—A—1

LITTLE IS known about the Courier Car Company of Dayton, Ohio. It was founded in 1909, capitalized at $200,000, a healthy start for those days. It faded away in 1915. Its production was probably several hundred vehicles a year at most. It is believed to have been owned by a member of the Stoddard family, builders of the Stoddard-Dayton automobiles from 1905 until 1913. The Stoddard-Dayton was made for wealthy mid-westerners, and a 1908 advertisement notes their Model 8 Limousine uses the "best grade of goat-skin, satin, and broadcloth, being complete with speaking tube, electric lights and toilet and cardcases."

The Courier Speedster was a lean and hungry-looking two-seater made with a different clientele in mind. The company's literature exhorted the buyer not to be flimflammed into buying more of a car than he needed. The bare look of the Courier certainly made a good case for that selling point. Where else could one get a dashboard without instruments? The driver of the Speedster was not to be informed about such things as oil pressure, engine temperature or even his actual speed. The wheelbase is a tidy 100 inches, tire size 32 x 3½ inches, and the four-cylinder motor produces 22½ h.p. Cruising speed is about 35 mph, ignition being provided by magneto and dry cell. Courier advertising made a virtue out of the car's modest power as follows:

> Railroad men don't use 8-driver Mogul freight locomotives to pull passenger trains. Don't *you* buy a car of greater power or capacity than you *need*. Let the other man pay for his folly. *You* get a "Courier."

If the original customer wanted to stay dry, he added $55 to the price of $1,050 f.o.b. Dayton, Ohio, for a top and top irons.

The condition of this Courier Speedster before restoration defies description. Fortunately Walter McCarthy, the owner, took the pictures before carting it home, which are reproduced here. It is not surprising that collectors had passed by the ruins of this motorcar for a period of ten years before Mr. McCarthy accepted the challenge. The major repair needed to the frame was to mend a

55

This car represents a test of the restorer's skill.

large break at the spring mount with heavy angle iron. Axles and side rails were sound but hood and fenders had to be replaced. Although rusted, enough remained of these to provide an accurate pattern. The huge three-quarter elliptic rear springs were pitted but sound. Wheels were respoked, and a search begun for the accessories needed, such as side and headlamps. An original factory circular gave details of running gear. Restoration was done over several years and the finished result so impressed Lester Cutting, who had sold the car to Walter McCarthy in the first place, that he bought it back.

Manifold side of Courier engine, from 1910 catalogue.

Carburetor side of engine, from 1910 catalogue.

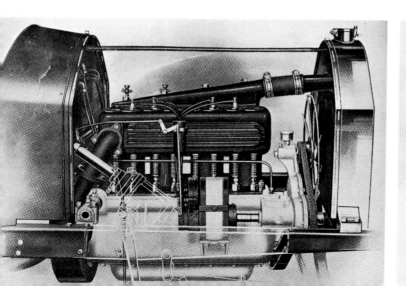

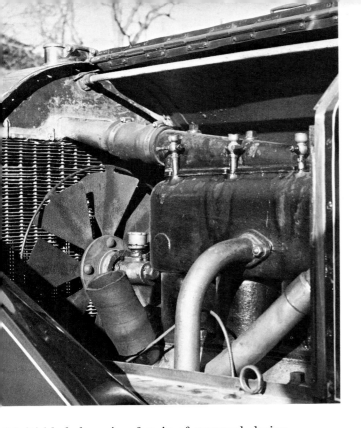

Multi-bladed engine fan is of unusual design.

The frame was basically sound although the steering wheel is missing and the ignition box, gutted. Note the H-slot transmission gear change which Packard had introduced a few years earlier.

Photo courtesy of Walter McCarthy

Ignition was by magneto and dry cell, mounted alone on the dash.

Compare this view with pre-restoration photograph of the same area of the cockpit.

Huge three-quarter elliptic rear springs could either be ground down or filled for a smoother finish.

In the testing-out of Courier cars there is no such thing as "general average." We make no boast as to how many Courier cars we are going to make in a season. Rather, we bank our reputation on the performance and efficiency of each car. The number of cars we build does not, cannot, bear any relation to the satisfaction that each Courier car must give its particular owner.

Our output is limited. Not by our factory capacity however, but by the absolute restriction that each car going out must bear, unqualifiedly, our fullest guarantee.

Railroad men don't use 8-driver Mogul freight locomotives to pull passenger trains. Don't _you_ buy a car of greater power or capacity than you _need_. Let the other man pay for his folly. _You_ get a "Courier"

Frame construction on the "Courier" is pressed steel; heavy gauge; channel section wide and deep; wonderfully rigid; rear springs ¾ elliptic; just sufficient to take up jolts and jars, but not so springy as to keep you going up and down, baby-carriage-like, continually; there's a happy limit in spring designing—you will find it on the "Courier"

Information given in factory literature is valuable when a car is in such poor condition that the location of parts is uncertain.

Seat and gas tank detail show simple mounts.

Details of differential and of a typical speedster gas tank.

Three-quarter view illustrates the unusual layout of the Kelsey Motorette. The body is painted black, with fenders, wheels, and seat in red.

1911 KELSEY MOTORETTE, MODEL M

THIS CONCEPT of a vehicle conceived to fit somewhere between a motorcycle and a four-wheel motorcar dates from an age when many car designers had open minds as to what the automobile should be like. A half dozen three-wheelers had been built and run prior to 1900, some operated by steam, others by gas. A few used the single wheel forward to steer and power the vehicle. Our Motorette is chain-driven by the single wheel at the rear, steering being accomplished by a conventional tiller coupled to the front wheels. The Leon-Bollee tricycle, which was being produced in quantity in 1897, convinced Mr. Kelsey that the "trike" was the car of the future.

Carl Kelsey was born in 1880 and in his student days lived in the suburbs of Philadelphia. Fascinated by engines, he studied steam and gas designs and spent his summer vacations as an apprentice in a machine shop. When he was seventeen, he built his first vehicle, a one-cylinder machine with a system of belts that, unfortunately, failed to move it at all. He sold the motor of this unsuccessful car and used the money to tour the automobile factories of Europe. This trip led to construction of a machine now in the Smithsonian collection known as "The Kelsey and Tilney Autotri." Though moderately successful as a vehicle, financial backing for manufacturing it was unobtainable and the car never saw production. From this venture in 1898 until the air-cooled model of the Motorette was brought out in 1910, Mr. Kelsey designed several other prototypes, always marked by novel features, and he also operated Locomobile and Maxwell agencies.

The Motorette designer anticipated a sure seller in the low-price field. Mr. Kelsey thought the Model T would monopolize the $800 to $1,000 car market, and he visualized a large sale for the two-seater Motorette at $385. To awaken the public to the virtues of the "trike," he sent one on a transcontinental trip, which, amazingly enough considering the primitive roads, was completed without undue difficulty.

Converting the original overheating air-cooled engine to water cooling improved performance. In an ambitious attempt to break into the big time, pro-

Photo courtesy of Robert Zlotoff

One of several boxes of parts photographed before the owner sorted and cleaned pieces of his Kelsey Motorette.

Two-cylinder engine of $3\frac{1}{4}$ x $3\frac{3}{4}$ inch bore and stroke is located under the passenger seat. Lines lead to oil valve located on seat front.

Oil-valve lever feeds o through four lines. The b houses the coil of the A water Kent Unisparker Ign tion. Plunger at lower rig is a compression release t facilitate starting.

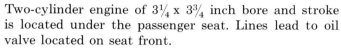

duction of 2,500 vehicles was planned for 1912. In order to keep costs down and speed up delivery, the motors were sub-contracted to another big company. This firm, unfortunately, was having production difficulties and in some way never explained, many of the engines were defective. This was not revealed in the brief tune-up each machine received at the factory and dozens were delivered to Motorette customers with a one-year guarantee. Most of the engines seized up in days. Although Mr. Kelsey and his sub-contractor labored hard to make good on every complaint, irreparable damage had been done. It is pointless, of course, but interesting to contemplate how things might have gone if the rugged engine built in the Motorette plant has been available for all the machines sold. The Motorette seemed to have a huge potential market as a low-cost passenger and delivery van. A few actually saw service in Japan as motorized rickshaws.

Mr. Kelsey went on to develop friction-drive cars of large size and elegance until the mid-twenties. He later founded and headed the Rototiller Company.

Removal of back cover reveals the rear of 10 h.p. engine and radiator hose.

Three floor pedals of Motorette are, left to right, brake, low and reverse.

Now in retirement, he recalls those early days in great detail. He even remembers which parts of the Motorette were pin-striped, and this colorful edging on the fenders and springs is exactly as it was originally.

The owner, Robert Zlotoff, knows of only one other restored Motorette in existence. That one, which is in the Henry Ford Museum, lacks the sway-bar feature. This stabilizing bar, an automotive first, is necessary to prevent the vehicle from overturning when rounding corners.

This 1911 Motorette was found in Millerton, Connecticut, and Mr. Zlotoff purchased it after five years of patient negotiation. The body had been dismantled and the fenders were suitable only for patterns. The engines and running gear were piled in several wooden boxes, which lent a Chinese puzzle aspect to the restoration project. Ironically, Mr. Zlotoff had almost completed work on the automobile when he located Mr. Kelsey, who helpfully supplied him with original literature and manuals on the Motorette. The nickel-plated "Jones" lights are authentic equipment and very scarce. Mr. Zlotoff swapped several old brass automobile lamps for them.

This superlative restoration has taken several major awards, including a National first from the Veteran Motor Car Club of America. Mr. Zlotoff drives the Motorette to local meets, usually within a thirty-mile range. Cruising speed is 20 mph, and the one startling characteristic the car has is a reluctance to climb hills at a pace over 5 mph.

64

The tiller is folded down so that the driver can climb into the car.

Detail of chain-driven rear wheel.

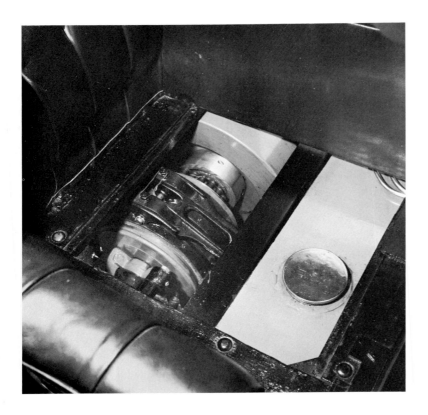

Gas tank and transmission are located beneath the driver's seat.

The two knuckles under the head lamp secure the stabilizer bar that steadies the vehicle on turns.

The Motorette was tried in other versions than the two passenger Model M shown. In a rickshaw version used in Japan the operator perched above the rear drive wheel.

The Panhard's massive appearance befits a car that in 1911 cost $4,350 for the chassis only.

1911 PANHARD AND LEVASSOR TOURING CAR

Knight Engine

PANHARD and Levassor, a French company, shares with Benz the distinction of being one of the two oldest surviving auto firms with an unbroken series of motorcars dating from the nineties. Noted for being the first to establish the general arrangement of the modern automobile, Panhard's placement of engine, clutch, gear shift system and the elimination of the popular belt drive provided a pattern of development for the next several decades. Monsieur Levassor, while hearing the grinding clash of gears from the primitive sliding pinions used in an early Panhard, remarked: "It's brutal, but it goes."

By the time of the Vanderbilt Cup races, Panhard was producing refined machines of great speed and durability, winning the 1904 event and taking second place the following year. By 1911 the company had established an American market for their cars based on power, prestige and luxury.

Panhard offered the Knight sleeve-valve engine, made under license, as an alternate choice to their poppet-valve motor. The Knight engine had a bore and stroke of 4 x 5½ inches, with four separately cast cylinders. In this type of engine, sleeves with ports cut in them have the function of valves, one around the piston and one inside the cylinder. They are operated by a timing crankshaft driven by a broad chain from the main crankshaft. This engine earned a reputation for actually improving with use. The higher cost of manufacturing the engine was reflected in the New York price (for chassis only) of $4,350, an increase of $150 over the poppet-valve model.

The tourer illustrated is the 30 h.p. model. It has two sets of brakes, the rear-wheel brakes being connected by adjustable steel ribbons instead of by the ordinary cables. Multiple-disc transmission was provided, featuring four speeds forward and reverse, high gear being direct drive. A cruising speed of 60 mph, giving almost fifteen miles to the gallon, was claimed, and the automobile does deliver that performance.

Walter McCarthy acquired this Panhard several years ago, tracking down

69

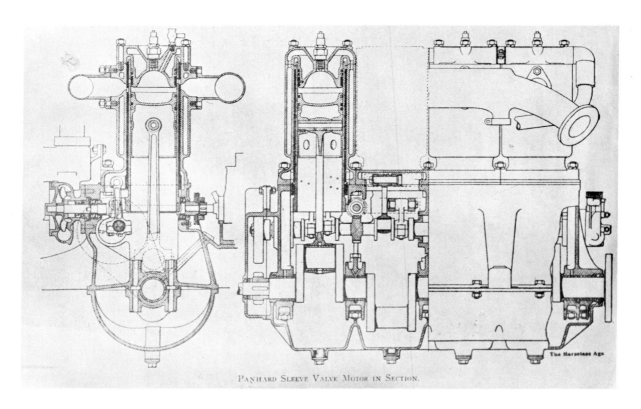

PANHARD SLEEVE VALVE MOTOR IN SECTION.

The Horseless Age carried this drawing when the Knight sleeve-valve engine was first used in the Panhard.

The high-tension magneto (at side of engine near fender) revolves bodily around its armature to advance the spark.

a lead provided by a fellow automobile club member. It is thought the car was from a collection of unrestored vehicles in Rhode Island. The car came with its two original bodies, a tourer and a limousine, but space restrictions forced Mr. McCarthy to part with the closed body.

The touring body was found to be solid, and in fact the leather upholstery is original. Mice had got into the top, and it has not been replaced, the automobile being run as an open car. The rear fenders were rusted out and required replacement. All brass lamps were missing, and Mr. McCarthy took pains to replace them with authentic units. The head lamps are Bleriots, made in Paris. The clock, horn and speedometer also were missing, and American made units were used, as the original car bodies were domestic. The hood and front fenders are plated with some kind of corrosion-resistant finish that has preserved the metal remarkably well. Early in the restoration process, which took about two years averaging thirty hours a month, one problem arose. The rear end kept binding, but this fault was finally traced to a bent pinion shaft. Mechanically the car presented no other difficulty and little had to be replaced. Even the splendid dash, thought to be curly maple, is original. Mr. McCarthy takes his family on extended tours in the Panhard and with its almost modern acceleration and comfortable cruising range of 55 to 60 mph, it presents no problems in traffic.

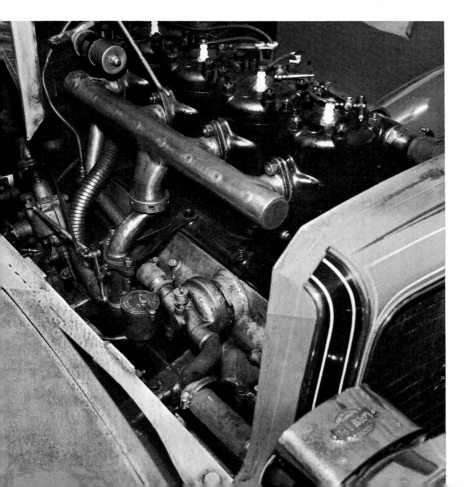

The same cross shaft that revolves the magneto (shown on the right side of the sleeve-valve engine) operates the water-circulating pump next to the carburetor. Note the four separately cast cylinders.

The cockpit of 1911 Panha

Twin sight-feed gauges for lubrication are unusual. One of these indicates oil going to the engine, the other, oil going to the transmission and clutch.

Solid twist controls on the steering wheel were used for spark and throttle.

Clean lines and one of the first of the early alligator-type hoods mark the body style.

The front view shows how much wider the top is than the windshield.

1912 CASE
TOURING CAR

FOR A MAKE that enjoyed a fine reputation for eighteen years (1909–1927) the Case automobiles are relatively unknown today outside of the midwestern states where they were most widely distributed. The J. I. Case Threshing Machine Company of Racine, Wisconsin, entered the automobile market in 1909 with a name renowned since Civil War days for the quality of its farm machinery. Its trademark, a scowling eagle with folded wings, grasping a globe in its talons, was inspired by a famous mascot of the 8th Wisconsin Regiment named "Old Abe." An early version of the emblem adorns the boiler of a portable steam engine built by the Case Company in 1869 that is now displayed in the Smithsonian Institution.

The Case was not made to a price or for a mass market. At $2,300 in 1912, this elegant tourer was definitely a quality vehicle, built to high standards. The company's slogan was "Case—The Sign of Mechanical Excellence the World Over."

In the ecstatic words of a 1916 ad-man:

> It is the Case that sets the pace
> It was a Case that won the race
> It is the Case whose motor, stability and grace
> Bring smiles to every owner's face
> It takes him where ere he wills
>
> It climbs with ease the steepest hills
> In the valley it runs smooth
> While every tired nerve it soothes
> The aged, the young, the ones between
> They ramble on with tranquil mien
> The grandest car 'twas ever seen.

Unfortunately, there are no records to indicate the results of this Olympian verse on the car-buying public of San Francisco, where this ad appeared.

A big year for self-starters was 1912. Such a device was beginning to be thought indispensable, and methods employed ranged from compressed air and electrical means to mechanical linkage and acetylene gas. Case elected to furnish its vehicles with the new Prest-O-Lite starter system. A separate tank was supplied for this rather complicated device, with a second cylinder on the running board furnishing the brass lamps with fuel.

This 3,000-pound car runs on $4\frac{1}{2}$ x 37 inch Firestone tires inflated to (ouch!) eighty pounds. The wheelbase is 120 inches and a low-tension magneto ignition is employed. The Case four-cylinder motor delivers 40 h.p., and the rear end was built by Timken-Detroit.

Our rare machine was found in Salamanca, New York, in 1960. The present owner and restorer, Charles Hartman of Massapequa, New York, followed up a tip passed along by a fellow antique car enthusiast who was in the throes of his own tourer restoration project.

The first inspection was discouraging. The car was in a barn, but at one period had reposed in a field for a good dozen years. The rear end faced a nearby hill, and local farm boys had made the carcass of the Case a target for their "varmit" guns. The metal was riddled with dozens of bullet holes.

Placed in the barn many years ago, the car had gradually sunk into the packed earth floor until the wheels were four inches down. All the demountable rims (and tires) were missing except for one spare. The body was tipped over sideways, having been detached from the chassis, and the front end was smashed in from a collision, the reason for laying the car up decades before. Surprisingly, when Mr. Hartman dug away the earth around the wooden spoked wheels, no rot was found. As the barn was leaning heavily on a huge tree trunk braced against its side, he lost no time in towing the Case out before the structure gave way.

After being taken to Massapequa, the body and engine of the Case were removed and the chassis stripped. Many hours with caustic soda, steel wool and a stiff wire brush followed. Loose rivets were knocked out and replaced with new hot rivets. Probing the differential revealed that the original lubricant had become a doughlike clay. This was spooned out and the unit flushed clean with kerosene.

Photo courtesy of Charles Hartman

The Case being taken out of the legendary barn.

The major restoration problem was to replace the missing demountable rims. As thirty-seven-inch Baker split rims are exceedingly rare, Mr. Hartman sought the help of the American Wheel and Rim Company of Newark, New Jersey. The company took a dozen or so smaller rims of the same width, which Mr. Hartman was able to find at old car flea markets, and made four Case replicas from them.

Mr. Hartman's restored Case has taken the family as far as Newport, Rhode Island, in comfort. The one alarming characteristic of this smooth-tired automobile is a tendency to get skittish on rain-slicked roads. This was hardly a problem in 1912, as the smooth tires were seldom matched to smooth roads.

The Case 40 h.p. four-cylinder cast-in-pairs engine.

Engine compartment and horn detail.

Spark and throttle levers are on the wheel.

The Bosch magneto switch is above Stewart speedometer, the handle at left is Prest-O-Start control. The small porthole between indicates oil level.

The beautifully detailed door has a map pocket.

The emergency brake nests behind the spare tire.

"Old Abe," the eagle adapted from a Wisconsin regimental emblem, indicates that Case products encircle the globe.

A rare accessory, a Neverout Taillamp with license plate bracket.

This tourer is maroon and black with yellow pin-striping.

The driver's side shows the tank for acetylene gas, the brake lever and the spare tire.

Note the ornate window design.

1913 DETROIT ELECTRIC
BROUGHAM, MODEL 42

ELECTRIC automobiles enjoyed a brief vogue in the early days of motoring up to World War I. It was the absence of two faults common to the gas cars of the day that made electrics popular, and when those defects were remedied, the gas cars surged ahead and electricity faded out of the propulsion picture. The defects were the lack of a self-starter and the noise and smell associated with the early gas engines.

Electrics were silent, totally silent in an almost uncanny way. Later models, like this 1913 Detroit, used a shaft drive, eliminating the noise of a chain drive, about the only noise they could make. The major disadvantage of the electrics was a driving range limited to about a hundred miles. The owner then would have to plug in the cable of his mercury-arc charger to restore the batteries. Detroit used Edison batteries while others, like Hupp-Yeats, used Exide products. The batteries usually comprised 27 or 30 cells and were huge and heavy, taking up all the space under the automobile's hood and rear deck.

A speed limited to 25 mph and a hundred-mile driving range were not severe handicaps to the matron of the day when trips around town might only total three or four miles. When people became accustomed to a day's drive, the electric became unreliable indeed. For a brief time these cars held a fair share of the market. Never inexpensive, they ranged in price from $1,700 to $3,000. The advertisements of the day usually portrayed a woman at the tiller, and the absence of heavy gears to change (and clash) and a massive wheel to turn appealed to the lady driver.

Driving this Detroit is simplicity itself. After inserting the ignition key, the brake is released with a firm kick on the cluster of three pedals on the floor. The long arm of the tiller is grasped by the right hand, the short lever by the left. This speed control arm clicks through five speeds forward, and after passing over a switch that reverses polarity, five speeds in reverse. As there are no gear changes, speed progression is silky-smooth as in a steam car. Milady minds her volts and amps, and speed, by peering at instruments located at

83

(*Opposite*) Three-quarter view indicates the excellent visibility this model afforded.

Rear battery compartment. Hatch covers were made of aluminum.

A 1911 advertisement cites improvements, particularly a direct gear drive, although the brougham shown has a chain drive.

her feet, presumably running off the road every once in a while. Why these dials were not brought up before the driver's vision is a mystery. The Detroit brakes are novel, separate pedals being provided for each rear wheel, which might account for rather erratic stops.

This product of the Anderson Carriage Company of Detroit is well preserved, with its original interior and its blue and black paint. Mr. Jorgensen, with the help of a battery expert from Exide, replaced the original dead cells with four-teen modern heavy-duty six-volt golf-cart batteries.

Mr. William W. Willock, Jr., who owned this machine from 1942 to 1961, had some much-envied pleasure drives in it during the gas rationing of World War II. He once raced the car at the Long Island Mineola Fair Grounds, a futile endeavor, as top speed of 25 mph could only be achieved downhill.

The charger that came with the car, an indispensable accessory for an electric, provided Mr. Willock with some anxious moments. It had been tampered with, and until Mr. Willock and a General Electric representative got together with an original instruction book, it would not charge. The unit consists of a large slate switchboard with meters, switches and a circuit breaker on the front, a large mercury bulb on the back, all this surmounting a huge transformer.

After plugging in the charging cable to a socket on the rear of the car, the circuit breaker and line switches are closed and the starting switch turned on. The next step is to rotate a knob that causes two pools of mercury to touch and start the arc. In Mr. Willock's words: "Immediately the starting switch was thrown down to run position, and away she went, with the tube full of blue fire, and humming like a hive of bees."

The Detroit Electric, Baker, Hupp-Yeats, and Rauch and Lang all passed out of the passenger car scene by the mid-twenties, but electric power for in-plant trucks and hauling continues. Electric delivery trucks left the streets of New York in the forties. Scarcely a decade passes without a major effort to bring back electric street vehicles. The rising menace of urban air pollution will perhaps provide the impetus to solve the old problems of heavy weight and short-lived batteries. The Edison Institute is working on a project to find the answers. If a solution is found and future motorists glide silently into spotless service stations to switch a depleted power pack for a fresh one, a relative hush may descend on our parkways. This will be a far cry, however, from the carriage house that the town small fry used to peer into at dusk, to watch the big "tube full of blue fire, and humming like a hive of bees."

Instruments indicate state of electric power in volts and amps. Warner speedometer included a tripometer. Right and left floor pedals control each rear wheel respectively, and center pedal is the parking brake.

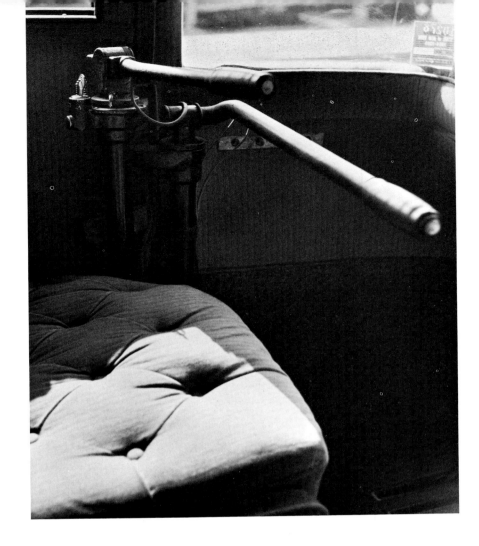

With the right hand grasping the long steering tiller, the left hand moving the short lever through the speed changes, driving the Detroit was simplicity itself.

The tufted upholstery is original and remarkably well preserved.

The jump seat next to the driver folds away when not in use.

Side lamps look like carriage
lanterns of an earlier era.

The 1913 Detroit Electric is credited with being the first production automobile to use curved glass.

Overhead view emphasizes the cane trim and clean lines of the car when the top is down and hidden in the lockers on the left and right of the rear seat.

1914 BENZ
TOURING CAR
Body by Schebera of Heilbronn

THIS EXOTIC machine, styled by someone with a passion for lifeboats as well as for automobiles, came from the Mannheim plant of Benz and Company in 1914. In their advertisements they stated forthrightly that they were "The Original Makers of Automobiles." Today few Americans realize that as far back as 1888 anyone had an actual factory producing automobiles in volume. Benz claimed 1883 as their first year of production, but 1885 would seem closer to actual operation of their little three-wheeler that developed three-quarters of a horsepower. Fortunately, this produced more actual motive power than a three-legged horse and was manufactured almost unchanged in large numbers for fifteen years. Even in 1888 the Benz plant employed fifty men.

It might be appropriate at this point to unravel the tangle of names concerning Benz. Benz and Company, Mercedes-Benz, Daimler Benz, the Mercedes Company, all stem from the two oldest German companies, Benz and Daimler. Daimler also founded the English company that supplied British royalty with cars of state for many years. The British company has thrived since its founding in 1897. Daimler, the German parent company, made its first motor carriage in 1886 and in 1901 resolved to change its Germanic name to improve sales in the French market. The Daimler representative in Nice was General Jellinek and his daughter's lovely name, Mercedes, was chosen. Benz and Mercedes went their separate ways until 1926, when they merged and became the company known since as Mercedes-Benz.

The Mercedes Company built large expensive machines in pre-World War I days. An interesting advertisement of the 1906 machine urges the reader to buy the American Mercedes, identical in every way except that it was built in Long Island City, New York. Cylinder castings, shaftings and forgings were imported from the parent company along with the shop drawings, and the car was duplicated here. It seems unlikely that anyone spending $7,500 for an automobile in 1906 would be concerned about saving the customs duty on the German-built Mercedes.

Like most European makers in the forefront of the industry, Benz and Mercedes were both active in prewar racing. Mercedes usually finished with the first five or six cars in early Vanderbilt Cup races, finally took second and third place in 1911 at Savannah, then a first in the Eighth Vanderbilt Cup Race of 1912. Their famed racer won again in this noted event in 1914 at Santa Monica, averaging 75 mph. In the seven U.S. Grand Prize races run between 1908 and 1916 at Savannah, San Francisco and elsewhere, Benz took second place three times and first and second in the 1910 event.

It is interesting to compare the performance of this 1914 mahogany-planked touring car with other cars of the period. In appearance its crowned fenders and smooth lines look more like 1925 than 1914. The material and workmanship in the car reflects credit on Benz. It is quite a modest performer however. The large and heavy body is on a chassis Benz described as a "light and powerful car." The cast-iron four-cylinder engine produces about 20 h.p. and has a bore of 3 inches. The speedometer is calibrated to 50 mph. and with a flawlessly rebuilt engine, maximum road speed is about 45 mph. One question arises repeatedly wherever the Benz is shown: Are the wheels fitted of the correct size? It is apparent in the profile view shown here that exceptional clearance exists between the tire and fender. The wheels are the original ones

The 1912 Benz did not have the famous pointed radiator.

After the car was stripped to the chassis, many hours with caustic soda and wire brush lay ahead.

and should be correct, but advertisements of the period show larger wheels more in proportion to the chassis.

The Mercedes-Benz people supplied Charles Hartman, the owner and restorer, with photographs of the chassis and a German language manual on the engine, demonstrating one of the fringe benefits available when restoring a car whose makers are still in business.

Mr. Hartman bought the car from a man in Bayshore, New York, who had nursed the idea of restoring the automobile since obtaining it in 1929. After bringing it home, the first step was removal of the body and restoring it in much the same manner as refinishing a lapstrake-type boat. The engine was removed and sent to a shop for an overhaul while the new owner worked on the chassis. The gas tank was rusted out and required replacement. A trip to upstate New York produced several yards of rare pyramid design aluminum for the floor. One of the headlights was perfect and one partially crushed. Because of its hammered design, a replica could not be spun of new brass. Mr. Hartman painstakingly hammered the shell and rim back into shape. The side running lights on the cowl have bevel-cut glass windows with blue-colored centers. As the technique for making this two-color glass seems to be lost, replacing one cracked lens has had to be postponed. Possibly inserting a blue center of plastic into an opening cut in a glass replacement and cementing with a transparent type of Epoxy resin might be a satisfactory substitute. The automobile was relacquered a jet-black. The hammered hood is nickel-plated over brass and with the trim of yellow caning brightens up an otherwise austere color scheme.

The major expense incurred in this restoration was the re-upholstering in leather of the huge body. Special compartments in the back of the front seat and the twin jump seats required extra work. The tool box on the running board is a replica made by Mr. Hartman, as is the huge Benz emblem adorning the cane-covered trunk. A close look at the wheel reveals it to be deliberately "squared-off," a feature Chrysler thought of in 1958.

With the disappearing top up, the automobile is a comfortable summer car with ample room for everyone except the driver, who is squeezed into a position cramped for anyone of even average build. This Benz won a first place at Hershey in 1965 for a newly restored car first shown.

Restored body mounted on the restored chassis.

Photo courtesy of Charles Hartman

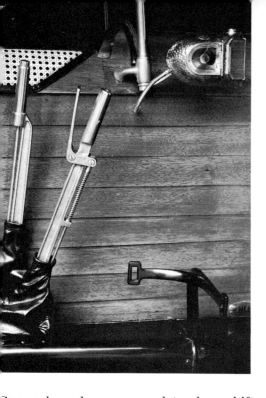

Spares have been removed to show shift
and brake levers. The levers were ground
down to remove heavy pitting.

The little cast-en-bloc four-cylinder motor takes
up about half the space under the hood.

The twin spares are in the running-board wells.

Looking down into the cockpit. Foot-pedal layout, left to right, is clutch, gas, and brake.

The crowned fenders have a modern look. Bumpers were not considered necessary in 1914.

Rear seat with jump seat folded out for use.

With its lofty top erected, the Benz presents a rather ungainly aspect from the rear.

Bumpers were usually not fitted on the Rolls-Royce in 1914. Dating an addition like this is difficult.

1914 ROLLS-ROYCE SILVER GHOST RUMBLE SEAT CLOSED COUPE

Body Builder Unknown

IF THERE is one legendary name against which every quality automobile built since the Kaiser's War has been compared, it must surely be Rolls-Royce of England. The car that created the legend was the machine that company offered in 1907. All its trim finished in nickel or German silver in the age of brass, its body enameled a silver gray, it was dubbed the Silver Ghost. Whether this was meant to refer to its color or its uncanny silence or a combination of both is a matter of conjecture. This model was so satisfactory in its performance and reliability that its production continued with only minor changes for nineteen years.

The two men who forged this company into the most respected automobile firm in the world could hardly have come from more divergent backgrounds. Henry Royce was born in 1863, the son of a miller, and was in turn a newsboy, railway workshop apprentice and machine tool worker. At sixteen he was working a sixteen-hour day. At twenty-one, after three years of hard work and study with the Electrical Company of Liverpool, he founded his own electrical products company. F. H. Royce Ltd. of Manchester thrived, and Royce products soon achieved a reputation for quality. Henry Royce bought a motorcar in 1902 and, in much the same manner as an American named Packard, felt the only way to express his dissatisfaction with his purchase was to build a superior car.

His third automobile, a light, exceptionally smooth-running two-cylinder machine, came to the attention of the Honorable Charles S. Rolls, wealthy son of an English lord. Rolls was an experienced racing driver and a salesman for some of Europe's finest makes of cars. He immediately appreciated the

97

potential of Royce's engineering ability, and Rolls-Royce Ltd. was founded in 1904. The two men experimented with several designs, including a revolutionary V-8-powered brougham, but it was their decision to market one large powerful model in 1907 that made their reputation unshakable.

Other companies might make excellent gears, only Rolls-Royce took every machined surface and polished the microscopic imperfections away by hand. Each chassis was test-driven hundreds of miles until every minor fault found was corrected. The gearbox, engine and radiator were mounted on sub frames to cushion their ride on the rough roads of the day. What astonished the motoring public was Rolls-Royce daring to announce, after winning the gold medal of the 1907 Scottish Reliability Trial, that they would run their Silver Ghost day and night until it had clocked 15,000 miles nonstop. The route was between London and Glasgow and the Royal Automobile Club certified the results. After an early fuel stoppage the Ghost ran nonstop for 14,371 miles. The total cost of repairs to restore the engine to as-new condition was about fifteen dollars.

The company went on to win major trophies and important trials. Contrary to a popular belief, the Rolls-Royce was not unconditionally guaranteed for life but for a period of three years. No other maker of the time could afford such a sweeping, all-labor-included guarantee.

The enormous six-cylinder engine of this coupe was cast in two blocks of three with side-by-side valves. Dual ignition using battery and coil and a separate high-tension magneto were used. Horsepower was gradually increased,

A 1915 advertisement shows a Silver Ghost. The text reflects the reputation the car had earned in less than ten years.

The flying lady, emblem of the Rolls-Royce from the period of the Silver Ghost.

with this model being rated at 48 h.p. at 1,200 r.p.m. Stroke had been increased to $4\frac{3}{4}$ inches. The biggest noticeable change was the replacement of elliptic rear springs with huge cantilever springs, which most body builders left partially exposed above the running board.

Richard Knies, the owner and restorer, has been unable to determine who supplied the closed body for his 1914 Ghost. He has only been able to trace the car back as far as 1925, when Inskip in New York sold it. The body style is similar to Brewster bodies of the period and although this body looks like a later model, patent plates on the door sills are dated 1915. It was common for used-car dealers of the twenties to update a valuable chassis with newer fenders, lights and bumpers, and it is possible that this was done. Beneath the present dash are cut-outs where the instruments were apparently located at an earlier date. The body is of aluminum on wood, with fenders of steel. The original mileage is not known, but it is believed that a 50,000-mile overhaul was performed by Rolls-Royce.

The car was put into storage in the late twenties and stayed off the road until 1950. It had been laid up again when Mr. Knies had the good fortune to hear of it, located just a block and a half from his home. He bought it in 1961 and restored it to its present attractive appearance. The Knies family participate in tours in their bright yellow Silver Ghost and have gone as far as the big annual meet in Hershey, Pennsylvania. The speed control feature works perfectly. The owner sets it at 45 mph and the Rolls-Royce dutifully maintains that speed uphill and down.

99

The big visor over the windshield adds to the car's exotic appearance.

The immortal 40/50 six-cylinder Rolls-Royce engine—the cylinders cast in two blocks of three, the crankshaft ground to one four-thousandth of an inch and carried by seven main bearings.

Fuel control petcock and brake adjustment knob above the running board.

Dash, thought to be a replacement of some ten years later.

Spark and throttle controls on the Rolls-Royce steering wheel, with the governor-setting control at left.

The huge rear springs of the Ghost are enclosed in "gaiters." Most body builders left the springs exposed.

The details of Rolls-Royce windshield are remarkably similar in appearance to those of 1923 and 1924 Lincolns.

One of twin dome lights in the passenger compartment.

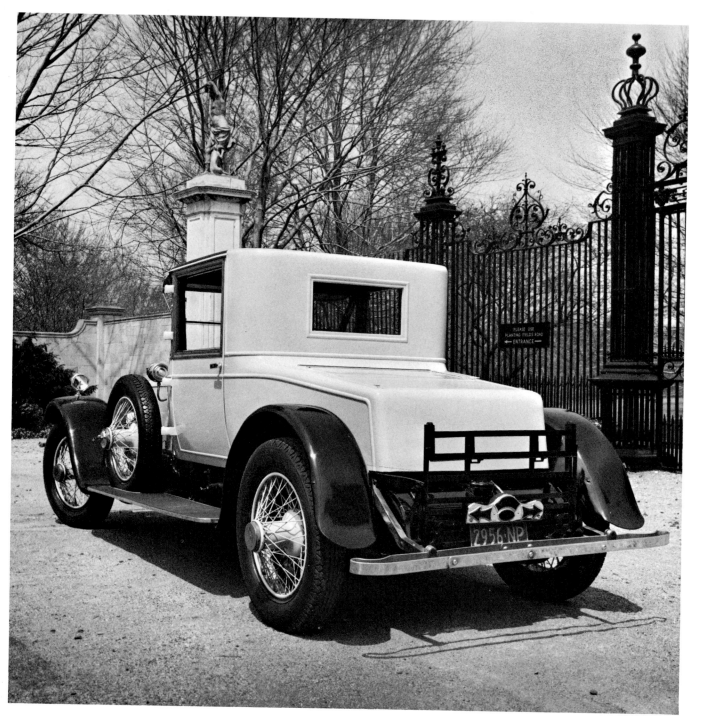

The angular body looks like a Brewster product but the maker is unknown.

1920 FORD,
MODEL T
CENTER-DOOR SEDAN

THIS FINE restoration is an interesting example of the best-known car ever made, "The Universal Car" as Henry Ford called it, the legendary Tin Lizzie. Its design and relentless production in overwhelming numbers catapulted the country ahead in two vital areas: the art of true assembly-line mass production and the growth of a nationwide road network. The appeal of the "T" was simplicity, low cost and reliability. Its success in terms of cars produced and sold was amazing. From something under 20,000 units made in the first model year of 1909, production soared to a quarter million automobiles in 1914 and crowded the million-car-a-year figure in 1920, when this sedan was made. Over fifteen million "T"s were built by 1927, when production lines in America, England and Australia were finally shut down, officially ending the longest run of an American model.

Ford profits in the twenties were reputedly about $50 per car. The 1920 center-door sedan illustrated here was considered "Top of the Line" at $975. The Runabout of 1925, for example, listed at the incredible price of $260. The average tourer or tudor sedan price remained in the $500 range for many years. Because Ford concentrated on building a basic automobile, thousands of small companies sprang up to supply the hundred and one accessories that owners' needs and Yankee ingenuity could dream up. These included dash-mounted starter cables to avoid wading out into the mud to "crank her over," electric light conversion kits for modernizing early models, and various-design shock absorbers to stabilize the "baby carriage" ride. Dozens of companies provided the buyer with speedster bodies, and many sporty-looking conversions were made.

This Ford was uncovered after decades of neglect when an old barn in Southampton, Long Island, was being torn down in 1962. John Sammons acquired it shortly after its owner had just begun the long restoration job it demanded. He installed it in his two-car garage, removed the body and worked from the

105

(*Opposite*) The spidery look belied the strength of the "T." The use of vanadium steel made Fords extraordinarily durable.

A 1925 advertisement. Ford was still selling the Model T on the wonders of the planetary transmission, which was unchanged since World War I.

chassis up. The engine block was rebored, the crankshaft turned down and a complete engine overhaul performed. Rusted-through fenders as well as fender aprons and hood required replacement. These were located in good condition on other "parts cars." The interior was completely redone with original-type material except for nonauthentic carpeting. The most unusual mechanical feature on the car was a Ruckstell rear end which converts the normal two speeds forward to four. Mr. Sammons was fortunate in locating a set of brand-new parts for this unit and was able to replace the badly worn original parts. This sturdy vehicle has taken the Sammons family on trips of a thousand miles and has logged over ten thousand miles since restoration was completed.

No automobile ever made has been the subject of as much discussion, debate, ridicule, adulation, aggravation, admiration and undying nostalgic affection as the Model T—certainly no other American car, at least. There is probably not a better description of the hold the "T" had on America's affections than these words of Stephen Longstreet from his *The Boy in the Model-T*:

> It was a much better car in many ways than those we had a few years later. It was simpler; it had no battery, no complicated wiring system, no automatic window-lifters or seat-movers to get out of order. We sat over the gas tank and measured it from time to time with a wooden ruler to see if we needed gas. . . . it was high enough to keep its crankcase from being broken by ruts, ditches, or low road crossings. It needed no brake fluids, special gasolines, greases or

doctored motor oils. A healthy man could lift it up by a corner for repairs. The fenders needed no expensive repairing, the body no specialist's body work. A jack could still fit under the car, and no chrome wheel shields, fancy locks, or a collection of many unneeded dashboard dials existed. In clumsy hands with nonmechanical minds, it ran well. Its illnesses were few, and the average citizen could attend to them with dime-store parts. If the radiator leaked, one dropped in a raw egg; the hot water soon sealed all leaks with hardboiled egg. . . . If a hill was too steep to climb, we turned the car around and went up it rearend first. It could crawl over rough ground. It could run for hours on a few gallons of cheap gasoline. It had handy running boards for standing on and attaching things to; it was high enough above the road so we could really see the landscape; and it bounced enough to give us the impression that we were really travelling outdoors, not in an air chamber underground.

The 20-h.p. motor that put America on wheels.

Rear end detail showing Ruckstell axle, traverse rear spring and battery mount on the body.

Front wheel detail shows double set of Hassler shock absorbers, a popular accessory.

Model T dash, a picture that many Americans would probably still draw from memory. The upper left floor pedal is the gearshift, two speeds forward; the center pedal is the reverse; and the one at the upper right is the foot brake.

Anti-theft accessory, the steering-wheel lock that prevented the wheels from turning.

Fender detail and tool box of the 1920 "T."

Interior of center-doo
sedan complete wit]
flower vase. The jum
seat next to the drive
folded out of the way

A side view of the 1920 Ford shows aptness of the model designation: center-door sedan.

Front view of the "T," showing Detroit Winter Front mounted on the radiator,
an accessory to improve the Ford's habit of hard starting in cold weather.

The classic Packard façade, a 1934 Le Baron.

5. THE CLASSIC CAR

WHAT does set apart a true classic from a standard production car? Two things in principal: brilliant and unusual design coupled with the most advanced engineering of the day. Almost inseparable from these attributes are two more basic factors: superlative hand workmanship and limited production. Some classics may excel in body design coupled to a lesser standard of engineering or vice versa, but all the above qualities are invariably found in a true classic.

There is general recognition by hobbyists of a golden age of motorcar design. This is the period of the twenties and early thirties. Many fine cars precede this period and others postdate it, but all the great marques were in their finest flower in these years. The leading authority from a collector's viewpoint in the designation of classic status in an automobile is undoubtedly The Classic Car Club of America. Their annual directory, revised and added to only after thorough analysis, lists those makes and models that meet the criteria of their definition of the term Classic. It would be unrealistic to expect every car lover to agree with every choice. It is hard to find a classic-car fan who hasn't a personal favorite he thinks has been overlooked. Their list is, however, a sound one and few will disagree with the vast majority of magnificent classic cars so designated by these knowledgeable automobile enthusiasts.

Many fine cars are of too recent vintage for inclusion in the era generally recognized as the classic age. At present these great machines have no well-defined status, the postwar automobiles built by Talbot, Salmson, Delage and such gems as the Bentley Continental and the 300 series Mercedes-Benz. Undoubtedly, in the years to come a category of modern classics will be recognized by some club and the elite of postwar automobiles will find an official home among collectors. These classic cars of the future will contrast sharply with cars of the golden age in at least two areas. Hand workmanship and custom

113

body building are virtually extinct and production has been and will be in such volume as to preclude scarcity.

One of the most attractive American cars of recent years has been described by British classic car experts Richard Hough and Michael Frostick as follows:

> . . . the Lincoln Continental regained its status in 1961, and the current model combines peerless beauty with standards of materials and finish that are matched by only one other motor car in the world. With the Phantom V Rolls-Royce, it maintains in purest form the standards of the great classics of the past, and no adjectival restraint whatever is called for in its description.

The interesting question is whether future admirers of this current Continental series will wish to preserve a car whose production surpassed a quarter of a million units. I believe the fine engineering and sheer beauty of design of this car will make it sought after in 1990 by collectors, as the high-volume, homely, but fascinating Model T is sought today.

Although fine machines of our recent past will undoubtedly be preserved, the term Classic will always seem most suited to the great machines of the golden age. Their hallmark will be recognized instantly in the gleaming stone guards, the sweep of racy fenders with side mounts encased therein, the glitter of wind wings and dual windscreens, huge landau bars and outsize trunks. The swift and silent passage of six thousand pounds of engineering genius and hand-crafted skills down a country lane will always mark the presence of a true classic, while a flying lady, leaping greyhound or soaring bird will proudly proclaim its maker's marque atop a gleaming radiator.

The Packard runabout with rumble seat open.

Minor dents on the fender edge are the only marks on the body of this sporty runabout.

1926 PACKARD RUNABOUT, MODEL 326

IT IS now a well-known legend that the Packard automobile began as a result of a peevish retort by Alexander Winton to his twelfth customer, James W. Packard. The year was 1898 and the dissatisfied manufacturer of electrical goods from Warren, Ohio, was complaining bitterly about his new Winton's performance, when he was told heatedly to build his own if he thought he could do better.

One year later James and William Packard rolled out their first 12-h.p. "one-lunger." They showed their machine in the Madison Square Garden show in 1900 and sold three. What enabled Packard to build a reputation while losing money initially was the loyal support of Henry B. Joy and his circle of Detroit bankers. A Packard owner since 1902, Mr. Joy knew the worth of the car, and when the brilliant Jesse Vincent took over as chief engineer in 1910, the company was making money steadily.

From 1903 on the Packard was a large, powerful four-cylinder car. The new Model N of 1905 had a wheelbase of 106 inches, 50-inch rear springs, and its big four was able to maintain 50 mph uphill and down. At $3,500 it was definitely a luxury car. Automobile advertising in those days was usually crammed with every conceivable detail about the vehicle, practically including the number of bricks in the factory where it was made. It is an interesting reflection on Packard's prestige that a 1908 advertisement shows a picture of a limousine and the copy reads, "Packard, Ask the Man Who Owns One." No details, no claims, not even price were considered necessary to sell the Packard.

At a time when a six was thought to be the ultimate in engine size, Jesse Vincent launched, in 1915, the engine that was probably Packard's greatest achievement. This was the amazing twin-six, first 12-cylinder American production engine, the first to use aluminum pistons. Eighty-five h.p. from a motor of 900 pounds was startling and Model 125 carried a surprisingly low price tag of $2,600. In the next several years the twin-six kept Packard the leader of the motoring social world, with Cadillac's V-8 the only contender.

In the lean years after World War I, a big six was introduced and in 1923

This 1928 Packard advertisement emphasizes the features of the central lubrication system. Note custom model prices to $8,970.

the famous straight eight. All Packard sixes between 1925 and 1931 are recognized as full classics by The Classic Car Club of America, and this runabout is a typical example. The big disc wheels were a Packard trademark for many years in the twenties. The car weighs in at 3,458 pounds and the wheelbase is 126 inches. Bore and stroke of the engine is 3½ x 5 inches, developing 60 h.p. The rumble seat and golf bag compartment were essential features of the day.

The headlights and fender lamps are not authentic Packard equipment, although dating from the same period. They are Woodlites and would be welcomed by anyone restoring a Ruxton, on which car they were standard equipment. The original large-drum Packard lights are still plentiful and would present a distinct improvement over the Wood units, whose tiny reflectors give off a glow rather than a beam of light. The top is a fairly recent replacement and a curious note is the lack of landau bars which are on the eight of the period.

This Packard is a good example of an old-timer so dependable it was never laid up in its forty years of use. It belonged to a New England Packard dealer, who ran it until the late fifties for business. A collector who later owned it for several years turned to modern sports cars and sold it to John Linhardt. Few classics of this vintage could be found with so little needed to be done for a full restoration. Except for the addition of an electric fuel pump, the engine is original. A new set of 600 x 20 whitewalls, a repaint of an authentic color scheme, replating and a new leather interior are the major items required. The discovery of a fine car almost half a century old in this condition is always encouraging to the enthusiast who has seen one basket case after another.

118

Manifold side of the capable 60-h.p.
Packard six.

Easy restoration is obvious from
this view. The dash is complete, and
only firewall and side panels require
much work.

The original rug in the golf bag locker is useful as a pattern for replacement.

These wind wings are original and rare. The bevel-c glass is chipped and should be replaced with safety plat

A valuable set of Woodlites. They were not original equipment on this Packard, however.

Metal bows are in perfect condition, but the top is no thought to be authentic in cut.

Rear view shows the Packard taillight unit is intact.

Resemblance to the Hispano-Suiza is seen in this view. Vertical lines are louvers
of the Allen Radiator Shutter, which is manually controlled from the dash.

1927 ISOTTA-FRASCHINI, TYPE 8A

Super Sport Roadster, Body by Fleetwood

FOR SOME reason, perhaps because they are both hyphenated, continental-sounding, and mellifluous, the public frequently confuses Isotta-Fraschini with Hispano-Suiza. The classic car enthusiast may be occasionally embarrassed to confuse the two cars themselves at a quick glance. The front ends of both classic machines are similar, and much of the custom coachwork of the period bears a common stamp. Where each company traveled a unique road was in their engineering. To simplify, the Hisso might be given credit for developing the ultimate six, and the Isotta top marks for a superlative straight eight.

Starting cautiously in 1900, Cesare Isotta and Oresta Fraschini advanced in six years from a one-cylinder car to a six. In 1910 their most impressive "first," four-wheel brakes, was introduced. Like Hispano-Suiza, the Isotta-Fraschini firm underwent a revolution in modern metallurgy during the throes of World War I production. Their aircraft experience led to use of lightweight alloys in their postwar automobiles. The type 8, offered in 1920, startled the motoring gentry of Europe. It was immensely drivable, by the standards of the day. Like the later Packards, the low-speed torque developed by the 80-h.p. engine enabled the driver to stay in top gear most of the time. Add to this factor advanced four-wheel brakes and superior suspension and its immediate acclaim was understandable.

The 1927 Isotta-Fraschini pictured is a series 8A which designer Cattaneo first modified in 1924 in an effort to match the performance of the Hispano Monza. Dual carburetors, increased bore and stroke, and lighter engine parts helped achieve that aim. The owner, Joseph Gaeta, has attained 90 mph in this car, which weighs in at 5,200 pounds and that is a sporting performance indeed. Factory specifications give the engine a bore and stroke of $3\frac{3}{4}$ x $5\frac{1}{8}$

123

THE FUN OF OLD CARS

inches developing 130 h.p. at 2,600 rpm. The nickel chrome crankshaft is supported in nine main bearings. Aluminum alloy pistons and a three-piece aluminum crankcase help to keep weight down. The American-built Fleetwood body, one of two of this design, is on a shortened wheelbase chassis of 134 inches, a reduction of 11 inches from the standard wheelbase.

In 1927, Mr. Gaeta had a foreign car agency in New York City and sold this Isotta-Fraschini to a California customer. At the customer's insistence, Mr. Gaeta delivered the machine in person after a demanding cross-country drive. After approving his purchase, and at 18,500 1927 dollars it was quite a purchase, the new owner requested Mr. Gaeta to return the car to his New York residence. The return trip was even more eventful, the car breaking a steering knuckle in Kansas and almost being washed away by an Arizona flash flood. The beautiful aluminum body was not meant for the volleys of stones thrown up by the wheels on the infrequent roads where the Isotta-Fraschini could be run at 60 mph. First the ⅛-inch-thick aluminum fenders became dented, then stones actually tore through them. Fleetwood later installed steel liners inside the fender crown to absorb such blows.

Despite the daily round of fixing flats and eating dust, Mr. Gaeta developed a deep affection for the virile Isotta. When his customer tired of it a year and 25,000 miles later, he bought it back. From 1933 to 1947 the Isotta was laid up in the family garage. Mr. Gaeta overhauled it in 1947, and it has been running ever since. New rings, re-babbitted bearing and wrist pins, and a recent valve job comprise virtually all work done since the car was new. The engine turns at 1,600 r.p.m. when producing 65 mph on the highway today, and delivers a surprising twelve miles to the gallon. Mr. Gaeta has only one regret concerning his association with the mighty Isottas, he wishes he hadn't parted with the elegantly bodied Castagna-Isotta he once owned.

Changing tires and fixing flats had to be repeated several times a day on the grueling transcontinental delivery trip.

Joseph Gaeta waits in the car as his co-pilot and a farmer discuss the situation. Twenty men, several horses and a tractor were finally required to extract the Isotta-Fraschini from the sodden Arizona landscape.

Photos Courtesy of Joseph Gaeta

Severely functional in layout, the Isotta-Fraschini straight eight produced 130 h.p. at 2,600 r.p.m.

Twin Zenith single-choke carburetors are fitted to the big eight.

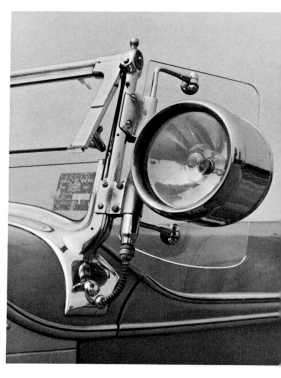

Dual spotlights are mounted on the wind wing

The cockpit of the Isotta-Fraschini features a dash recessed under the cowl. Only the shortest of drivers can see the upper instruments conveniently.

Louvers in the cowl are adjustable for ventilation of the driver's compartment.

The hood and cowl are silver, the body a pearl gray. The underbody is bright red.

Three-quarter view shows the rakish lines of fenders. The tool box is concealed in the running board.

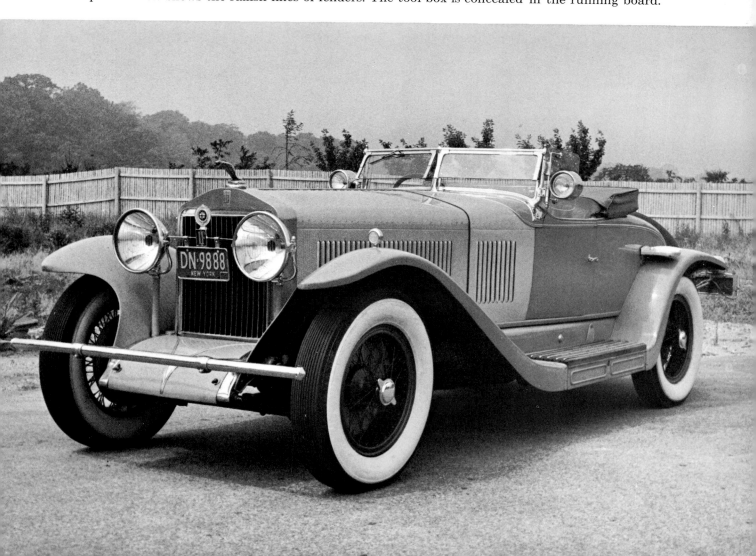

1929 HISPANO-SUIZA,

Country Model, American Type
Imperial Cabriolet,
Body by Hibbard and Darrin, Paris

THIS 1929 Hispano-Suiza is a striking example of how a great classic may come on the market at a reasonable price. The car shown has not been restored and these pictures indicate the restoration to be done. The extraordinary thing is how little work was required to put this machine back on the road after standing idle under covers for twenty-three years.

This model 37.2 was built to order in the French plant of Hispano-Suiza in 1929 for the Grace family of steamship-line fame. In those days a Hisso chassis cost about $13,000, with a custom body by Europe's finest designers adding another $5,000 to $8,000. This cabriolet body by Hibbard and Darrin, with a three-position top, was typical of the elegant styles available. The car was delivered for $16,400, including a trade-in allowance on a practically new 1928 Marmon roadster. Two pages of the contract described in detail exactly what custom accessories were to be fitted, and samples of apple-green leather in two shades were provided by the buyer to be matched.

The car was advertised in the classic car columns of *The New York Times* in 1961. It had been inherited by a member of the Grace family, who invited bids on the machine. Mr. Magnuson was the high bidder among fifty, and the Hispano-Suiza was his for a nominal sum. It is possible that the body style confused some potential buyers, who assumed it was a fixed-roof town car. Had the top been exhibited folded down, the car might have aroused more interest. (Folding the top down, however, would probably be disastrous, as the leather has age-hardened considerably.)

Work performed to date has included replacement of some electrical wiring, and relining of the brakes. A reproduction of the Flying Stork mascot was ordered, because unfortunately the original was stolen at some point before the car was towed home. A set of new tires was bought. Ultimately working toward full restoration, Mr. Magnuson, the owner, and his son plan on new

129

(*Opposite*) This view indicates the extraordinary care this Hispano-Suiza must have had. Although the bumpers require replating, they are unmarked.

upholstery in the chauffeur's compartment, refinishing the well-preserved leather in the passenger compartment, a new top and minor replating through-out. The major item will be a re-lacquer paint job up to Hispano-Suiza stand-ards.

This car is a tribute to Marc Birkigt, the Swiss-born electrical engineer who founded the Hispano-Suiza Company in Barcelona in 1904, and who is probably least known of the handful of first-rank figures in the classic car epoch.

Limited to the electric locomotive field in his native country, Mr. Birkigt was able to secure financing in Spain, and his budding company entered the luxury car market about the same time Rolls-Royce introduced the Silver Ghost in 1907. When the King of Spain organized a major race for the Catalan Cup in 1909, a Hispano-Suiza entry was mandatory, as it was the only Spanish-made automobile to represent His Majesty. The only car to finish other than the winning Lion-Peugeot, the Hispano-Suiza went on to win several important races before the Great War, establishing a record for durability.

Marc Birkigt designed a V-8 aircraft engine that powered most of the Allied aircraft flying during World War I. Over 50,000 of these engines were built in dozens of plants scattered around the world. In 1919 Mr. Birkigt borrowed from the design of this engine to power his best-known automobile. One bank of the V-8 design was increased to six cylinders and given a bore of 100 mm. and a stroke of 140 mm., the resulting engine developing 135 brake-horsepower

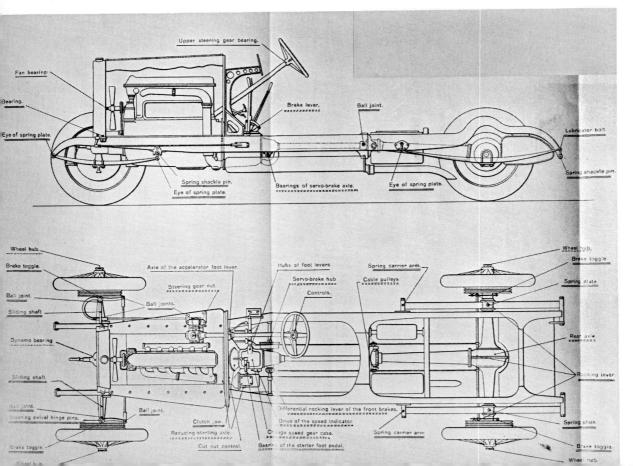

Factory lubrication sheet shows the massive scale of the chassis of the 37.2 Hispano-Suiza.

at a lazy 2,600 r.p.m. The engine peaks at 3,200 rpm and when cruising in the automobile here shown at 80 mph, the tach indicated 2,800 r.p.m. The car was distinguished by a remarkable power servo-brake system years ahead of its time, which Rolls-Royce saw fit to use under license. With a wheelbase of 145 inches and a weight just under three tons, performance is astonishing. Once in high the machine can be slowed to a crawl and then smoothly and swiftly brought up to speed without using the gears. Idling at rest, the engine is rock-steady, barely indicating it is running.

Marc Birkigt died in 1953, but the last of the great Hissos, a huge V-12, were made only into the late thirties. The company still thrives, fully wedded to the jet age in a variety of products, including liquid fuel rockets and nuclear power equipment.

In its day only the Isotta-Fraschini and Rolls-Royce were comparable, and many consider the Hispano-Suiza an automobile never outclassed. Michael Arlen in his novel *The Green Hat* fixed the Hispano-Suiza forever in its time and place with the following flight of prose:

> Open as a yacht, it wore a great shining bonnet; and flying over the crest of this great bonnet, as though in proud flight over the heads of phantom horses, was that silver stork by which the gentle may be pleased to know that they have just escaped death beneath the wheels of a Hispano-Suiza as supplied to His Most Catholic Majesty.

Illustration from a factory manual shows 99-pound crankshaft that was hewn from a 700-pound block of finest steel.

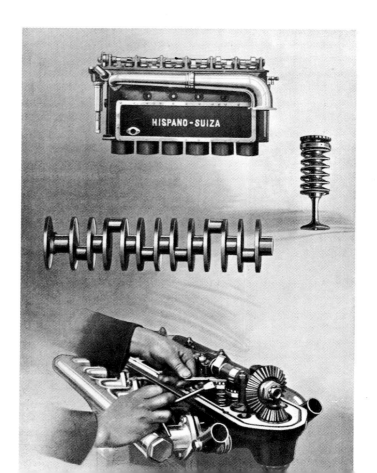

Manifold side of the 135-h.p. six-cylinder engine. Note corrosion-proof enamel finish on the upper half, a patented Hispano-Suiza process. This finish was apparently immune to time and chemical action.

The double-choke Hispano-Suiza Solex Carburetor is in the center; each barrel feeds three cylinders. The beautifully finished casting at lower left is the steering gear box.

By special order this Hispano-Suiza was equipped with arm slings as well as with passenger assist straps. The cameralike object below is an ash tray and built-in lighter.

The passenger compartment has one jump seat facing sideways and next to it, shown closed, a foldout writing table.

The chauffeur's compartment is the only part of the car showing wear. The leather is worn and cracked, and door sills are worn to the brass. The instrument panel is perfect, however. The gear shift gate, which is not in the traditional "H" pattern, calls for attention on the driver's part.

Monster 16-inch brake drums were equipped with hardened iron liners. Alloy castings on the liners were finned for rapid heat dissipation.

Tremendous Marchal headlamps gave more light than modern sealed-beam units. Grand touring in the twenties often meant driving on unlit mountain roads, and Marchal lamps delivered the powerful illumination necessary.

With a wheelbase of 145 inches, Hibbard and Darrin managed to give a graceful as well as a massive look to this three-ton machine.

1931 ROLLS-ROYCE
PHANTOM II CABRIOLET

Special Body by Taschmann-Inskip

IN 1926, Rolls-Royce closed out production of the legendary Silver Ghost after a run of nineteen years. The first of several "Phantoms" to replace it had a slightly larger engine capacity than the Ghost, developing about 100 h.p. In 1929 the Phantom II was introduced. Engine performance of the famous six was upped to 120 h.p., but the entirely new chassis was the big news with semi-elliptic rear springs fitted. Chassis weight was around 3,800 pounds, but performance reportedly equaled the current Isotta.

In order to match the performance of the Hispano-Suiza and come near the Duesenberg "J" figures, a lighter, shorter Phantom called the Continental was manufactured. Compression was 5.25:1, and the rear springs beefed up to take high-speed touring on poor roads.

The testing sequence Rolls-Royce engines and completed chassis were subjected to would make a contemporary American automobile maker blanch. After passing twelve hours' running in to prove out the engine's matching its specified horsepower curve, it was mounted in a chassis and a simulated ride at a wide-open throttle setting for an hour over revolving steel rollers took place. After passing this and other tests, everything was checked over again and the engine decarbonized before final installation.

The Phantom II chassis had an automatic lubrication system, each part receiving oil by meter according to its needs. This was carried to the extreme of grooved oilways provided between every leaf of the springs, all fed by the central system. The dual ignition system was a cardinal principle of Rolls-Royce thinking, and on the Phantom one set was by coil and battery and the other, on the opposite side of the engine, by magneto serving another six spark plugs.

The master body builders of Europe and America fitted the Rolls-Royce with their finest work. When the Phantom II was introduced, J. S. Inskip ordered

137

(*Opposite*) The Inskip-built body of this PII Rolls-Royce equals the finest coachwork of the period.

one hundred equipped with left-hand drive, and over the next few years had them fitted to the customers' orders. Most of these Phantoms had bodies built by the noted Brewster Company.

The Rolls-Royce illustrated, which is now owned by Philip Wichard, was originally fitted with a Brewster Keswick limousine body. In 1939 a new custom body was designed by Taschmann for the long wheelbase Phantom II chassis and was mounted on this chassis to the order of Joseph Morgenthaler. Mr. Morgenthaler was accustomed to the larger Rolls-Royce, trading in his 148-inch-wheelbase Springfield Silver Ghost. The former owner recalls driving the Phantom as a pleasure as long as one remembered to double-clutch. The synchromesh gearbox was not introduced until late 1932.

Designer Taschmann had designed automobiles for Diamond Jim Brady. The lines of his design have led many who see the car to describe it as the most beautiful Rolls-Royce ever made. The enclosed rear wheels are unusual on any Rolls. The color scheme is beige above fenders of deep claret. The body is of aluminum, with fenders of steel. The style is one of a kind, and its original cost was probably in excess of $20,000, a sum befitting the car whose slogan is: "The Best Car in the World."

The side-mounted spare wheel on this Taschmann-designed body is carried well forward, adding to the impression of length.

Spark, throttle and governor controls are almost the same as on the 1914 Silver Ghost.

Elegant cockpit of the Phantom II. Note the two switches for dual ignition.

Deep-set Rolls-Royce grill is flanked by fully crowned fenders.

The extreme rake of the rear end is evident in this view.

1931 LaSALLE
FLEETWOOD ROADSTER,
MODEL 345

THE LaSALLE was first introduced in 1927 as part of General Motors' developing practice of providing a line for every price range. LaSalle was to be a junior Cadillac, filling a niche between that luxury automobile and the middle-price-range Oldsmobile. It should be remembered that even a junior-grade Cadillac in 1927 must be a quality car in engineering, performance and finish. Priced from $2,300 and up, the LaSalle was offered in eleven body styles on 125 and 134 inch wheelbases. At the time a Willys Knight six cost less than $1,500, a Dodge six $800 and the Studebaker prestige leader, the President Eight Roadster, about $1,800. The LaSalle had to be good to succeed, and with a body styled like a small Hispano-Suiza, it was. Designer Harley Earl had given it a European appearance and General Motors engineers had provided a chassis having the virtues of the bigger Cadillac. Over a four-month period a dozen stock LaSalles racked up a third of a million miles at the proving grounds in an amazingly successful endurance test.

The life span of the LaSalle was relatively short, considering its early popularity, ending a thirteen-year series in 1940. Checking the data on each year's model and cross-checking with the category accorded by The Classic Car Club of America would seem to indicate a decline from a true classic car to a mere production automobile. Styling of all LaSalles was consistently attractive, but from 1934 on economies were practiced due to a slump in sales, which resulted in the car losing its original distinction. Olds engines were used until the market allowed the Cadillac power plant to be employed in the 1937 LaSalle once more. In 1941 it was a choice of upgrading the LaSalle again or creating a lower-priced model carrying the Cadillac nameplate. It seemed safer to market the 61 series Cadillac and bury the LaSalle.

Philip Wichard purchased this beautiful Fleetwood roadster from the original owner in 1963. It had not been run in a decade and was in fair to poor condition. Several of the authentic accessories like the running board mounted lights and the Pilot Ray lamp that turns with the front wheels were located

143

(*Opposite*) This head-on view illustrates why some thought the design of the LaSalle was inspired by the Hispano-Suiza.

THE FUN OF OLD CARS

through automobile hobby advertisements. Restoration required a year and was carried to the ultimate limit. Painting the trunk, for example, required expert consultation to solve an electrolysis problem caused by the juxtaposition of aluminum, brass and steel. The car has been driven on long trips, including two that brought home National first place awards from meets of the Antique Automobile Club of America and the Classic Car Club of America.

The exceptionally beautiful dash of the LaSalle roadster

Those who believe the engine to be a Cadillac power plant are right. The 90-degree V-8, displacing 303 cubic inches, powered the 1927 LaSalle and, increased slightly in power, was used until the cost-cutting days of 1934.

The side view shows the outsize trunk in true perspective.

A unique accessory: the Pilot Ray lamp, which, mounted on the crossbar, turns with the front wheels.

Chrome covers on the side mounts and the running-board spotlights add dash to an impressive classic.

Note the large trunk and the arm rests in the rumble seat of this LaSalle roadster.

Headlights that swept out of the fender in a continuous flowing line were a
Pierce Arrow trademark from 1914.

1931 PIERCE ARROW, MODEL 42 CONVERTIBLE COUPE

IN THE EARLY days of the classic age, a trio of great automobiles was affectionately referred to as the three "P's." They were, of course, Packard, Peerless and Pierce Arrow. At car meets today a Peerless is a rarity, a Pierce Arrow seen only slightly more often and the Packards arrive in droves. What the Pierce Arrow lacks is availability. Pierce's greatest classics were produced from 1930 on, when the company was literally dying. Its finest achievement, the V-12 of 1932, found no quick market because of the depression. In 1933 Ab Jenkins drove a stock roadster powered by the V-12 for over twenty-five hours, averaging an incredible 118 mph. The Pierce Arrow reputation was founded principally on stamina. The flexibility to look ahead and sense trends was not one of Pierce management's strong points. In 1916 eighteen firms offered V-8 designs, yet Pierce stayed with its big six until Studebaker took over control in 1928.

Founded in 1901 by George N. Pierce, the first car bearing his name was a one-cylinder motorette similar in appearance to many other machines of the day. He soon added a novel feature, moving the gear shift lever to the steering column. His automobiles grew rapidly in size, power and reputation. The Pierce Great Arrow of 1905 won the demanding Glidden tour, then repeated that success every one of the succeeding four years. The Great Arrow offered in 1908 was an enormous machine with three seats, a big six that developed considerably more than its rated 60 h.p. and carried a thumping price tag of $6,500. In 1914, with the advent of streamline body design, Pierce put the headlamps in the fenders and established a trademark that persisted up to the very last design in 1937. In the years of the Kaiser's War the public quickly forgot the nickname Fierce Sparrow that some unknown wit had applied to the early Motorette. The Great Arrow built such a name for itself people no longer thought of George N. Pierce as that bird cage manufacturer from Buffalo, but as a great car builder.

Never a style setter and unwilling to move up to eight or more cylinders, Pierce Arrow floundered in the late twenties, eventually becoming a subsidiary

149

of Studebaker. The Pierce Arrow name was retained and, fortunately, the engineering staff. This staff had a fine straight-eight engine ready and it was introduced in 1930, just a few years too late. With a bore and stroke of 3½ x 5 inches, this 385 cubic inch engine utilized nine main bearings, developing 132 b.h.p. Coil, points and condenser were in pairs, allowing the engine to run on four cylinders should one ignition part fail. Although Studebaker eights are similar, each was apparently developed separately, South Bend possibly picking up a detail or two from the Pierce men in Buffalo. The 1932 V-12 Pierce engine was a match for anything around, and it finally took style honors when the Silver Arrow was unveiled at the 1933 auto shows. Designer Philip Wright had come up with a dazzling beauty which unfortunately cost $10,000 per edition. Just when Packard was preparing to leap into the low-price market with both feet, Pierce was electing to survive with a quality car for the wealthy. There were just not enough buyers in that market, and the company staggered along on dwindling sales until 1937. In 1938 its name and assets were auctioned off for the appalling sum of $40,000, shortly after a prediction of 25,000 1938-model Pierce Arrows priced at $700.

Donald Gilbert heard of this Pierce through an advertisement in *The New*

The Pierce Arrow straight eight could keep up with anything of its day. Bore and stroke were 3½ x 5 inches. Displacement was 385 cubic inches.

Door detail of the 1931 convertible coupe shows the fine workmanship of the upholsterer. Note twin door guides, which give rigidity.

York Times in 1960. Driving out to a Philadelphia suburb, he was ushered into a small one-car garage. The Pierce Arrow was in exceptional condition, having run less than 40,000 miles since delivery in 1931. The seller, who had purchased the car from the estate of the original owner, believed it had never been operated in winter. A set of Pierce Arrow chains in a sealed factory bag in the trunk seemed to corroborate this. The beautiful body, similar in style to Le Baron or Murphy, is strictly Pierce Arrow, built in the Buffalo factory on the 142-inch-wheelbase chassis. It had cost $4,110 new in 1931, and it was equipped with the four-speed transmission Pierce Arrow favored.

Mr. Gilbert did not hesitate to buy this gem at the price of $1,100. He returned to Long Island for a co-pilot and then went back to take delivery of his acquisition. The five-hour trip brought only a slight protest from the Pierce Arrow, in the form of overheating. Mr. Gilbert has replaced the clutch and performed a valve job. The body was repainted, the chrome replated, and the leather interior redone. Steam-cleaning the chassis revealed the enamel finish on the running gear and bottom pans to be as new. A new set of 700 x 18 tires completed the job, probably setting some sort of record for minimum work required for maximum results. Only the arrow on the mascot was missing.

When viewing the solid quality of this fine machine, one reflects on what Pierce could possibly have brought out for $700. As it was, the reputation of the Pierce Arrow was never marred by such an impossible undertaking and continued unblemished to the end.

151

The uncluttered dash of the Model 42 is attractive.

A limited portion of the car's length is devoted to the passenger compartment. This is a feature of early classics in two-seater models. In this Pierce Arrow it is doubly apparent, due to the long 142-inch wheelbase.

The spacious rumble seat is opened by a tripping lever behind the driver's seat. The heavy hatch is spring-loaded and opens like a medieval catapult.

A rear view shows the Pierce's severely simple lines. The rumble seat hatch has no outside handle.

Special windshield trim and a special hood ornament were created for this 1934 Packard show car.

1934 PACKARD TWELVE CLOSED COUPE, MODEL 1106

Custom Body by Le Baron

FROM THE massive, squared-off road cars of the twenties, Packard entered the thirties with changes in style that were both sweeping and subtle. The Parthenon-like classic grill was still immediately identifiable, but the lines flowed more gracefully each year. Packards of the forties actually look higher, boxier and more dated by comparison to these beauties of the early thirties. The decade was ushered in by the Model 734 Speedster. Only a dozen or so survive from the hundred twenty-five Packards made for the country club set. From here on Packard built only eights in two lines. The Super eights developed 120 h.p., and the roadsters and convertible sedans of this period are impressive, the chassis being provided with as long a wheelbase as 145½ inches.

In 1932, the company sought to halt falling sales with a dazzling new model. After toying with the idea of making a front-drive car, it introduced instead a potent new V-12. Obviously, it wished history to repeat itself and restore the salad days of 1915 when 25,000 people crowded into one Packard showroom in forty-eight hours to view the first highly successful twin-six.

This new V-12 developed 160 h.p. at 3,200 r.p.m., having a bore and stroke of $3\frac{7}{16}$ x 4 inches. The 446 cubic inch engine was capable of actually starting off the 5,000-pound car in second gear. In 1935 its output was increased to 175 h.p. Production of the 12 ended in 1939 with a total run of almost six thousand units. This probably exceeds the total of other 12's like the Pierce Arrow and Marmon and the V-16 Cadillac added together.

All the great body builders worked on the V-12 chassis, including Derham, Brunn, Dietrich, Locke and Waterhouse. The model illustrated is perhaps rarest of the rare. For the 1934 automobile show Packard commissioned Le Baron to execute a McCauley design on the V-12 chassis. Nine machines were built, including three roadsters, three sport phaetons on a 144 inch wheelbase, and

155

three closed coupes on the 135 inch wheelbase. There was allegedly a dispute over who was to receive credit for the finished vehicle and the only body plate, on the door sill, states "Custom Made by Packard." These nine exhibition show cars cost Packard in the neighborhood of $18,000 each, and after they had served their purpose they were sold for $10,000 apiece. John Lindhardt, the owner of this Packard, has made an effort to trace the whereabouts of the other cars and apparently his coupe is the sole survivor of that model. One caught fire from a faulty muffler one night in the backwoods of Tennessee and the unfortunate collector, who had been driving it, saw it burn up before his eyes. The other coupe was the property of a Frenchman and it was destroyed in a World War II bombing raid. The Harrah Auto Collection owns one sport phaeton and a television personality another. The fate of the three roadsters is unknown.

All specifications of this machine are outsize: the water pump circulates forty quarts by means of twin-V belts, the engine fan is a six-bladed, twenty-inch-span aluminum brute, the crankcase takes ten quarts of oil and the fuel

The well-finished V-12 had domed and plated nuts.

The neat instrument console is set in dash of Carpathian elm trimmed with American walnut. The speedometer is calibrated to 120 mph and tachometer is incorporated in the same dial.

tank thirty-two gallons of gas. Moving a lever under the dash adjusted the orifice area of each shock absorber, allowing a soft or stiff ride, depending on the driver's wishes and the road. This ride-control feature and the Bijur central lube system were standard on the 12.

Registered every year, this rare Packard was purchased by Mr. Lindhardt from the original owner. Total miles in thirty-one years was eighty-eight thousand, and a major overhaul by Packard had been performed on the V-12 in 1950 at a cost of $500. In 1953 a properly executed paint job was done, involving the removal of the fenders, doors and running boards. Nineteen coats of hand-rubbed Valentine lacquer were applied, and after fourteen years it still looks new.

Mr. Lindhardt plans to mount new whitewalls on his cream-colored twelve, and to have new rugs made for the interior. The only work required on purchase was to remove the ugly sealed-beam conversion and to remount the original lights, which the owner had fortunately preserved.

This machine properly belongs in that exclusive company of "idea" cars like the Pierce Silver Arrow of 1933. Whether styling like this on production 8's would have helped Packard sales is anybody's guess. Packard kept afloat after 1935 with the low-priced 120 and 110 series. The company also gave away the priceless prestige associated with its famous grill. Wartime profits gave the firm a second chance to recover its share of the market, so it does not seem entirely fair to blame its demise on the 110's. Innovations like the Ultramatic transmission and then the load leveler of 1955 had bugs that further hurt the Packard's reputation. The 1958 Studebaker sedans that masqueraded behind a Packard emblem, with a supercharger tacked on for glamor, caused Packard fans to turn away with a shudder. Packard's golden age definitely ended in the thirties, but how many makers could claim a reign as long and glorious?

157

Airplane design influenced automobile stylists in the thirties and may be the inspiration for the winglike window treatment.

The door arm rest, as well as ash tray and dome light, has a teardrop shape.

The profile emphasizes the teardrop styling and the pontoon fenders.

The three-quarter view marks the twelve as unmistakably Packard.

The custom rear wheel covers had a Packard twelve emblem.

Front pontoon fender actually wraps around and beneath the running board. Engine louvers are reminiscent of the Duesenberg.

The fast-back treatment and the small window make fender mirrors necessary.

Low angle view of a classic nose. Oblong lamps on the bumper are later-day additions.

1934 MERCEDES-BENZ 500K CABRIOLET, STYLE B

THIS impressive car marked an historic turning point for the German firm of Mercedes-Benz. Until 1934 the company had always led with a pure performance car as its highest-priced prestige automobile. The 500K was a touring car, of fine performance undoubtedly, but not the ultimate in speed. The five-liter engine powering this Mercedes was developed from the 3.8-liter engine introduced in 1932. One of the most deceptive things about its racy appearance is that the low four-passenger body camouflages a car weighing 5,440 pounds. The wheelbase is a comfortable 129½ inches. When the hood is raised and the enormous engine is viewed, filling every inch of space, it becomes apparent that this machine is no lightweight. The massive frame seems a portent of Dr. Porsche's future work on the eighty-ton Tiger tank. The car employs four-wheel independent suspension on coil springs, and the hydraulic brakes are vacuum-assisted.

The 500K series was considered to be sluggish in comparison to the previous S series and the SSK machines that had been sweeping to victory in so many of Europe's top races of the late twenties. The ultimate sports machine Mercedes developed in this period was undoubtedly the SSKL. Its frame perforated from one end to the other to reduce weight, its high-performance engine produced 300 h.p. with the huge "Elephant Kompressor" cut in. It could attain 150 mph on a straightaway, and had the current Bentley met the Mercedes in a series of races, the outcome would have been exciting to say the least.

Acceleration in this Mercedes is not startling by modern standards, but once up to road speed it gives the impression that touching the 100 mark would be quite possible. The Roots type Supercharger (or Kompressor) is engaged by flooring the accelerator. The blower pumping air into the carburetor accounts for the banshee scream the Mercedes racing fans love. It is meant to be used for short bursts of extra power and on this model the specifications claim a jump from 100 bhp to 160 bhp with the blower cut in. The owner's son, Jeff Magnuson, took me on an interesting drive along the winding, hilly roads of

163

THE FUN OF OLD CARS

Long Island's North Shore and on a slight grade cut in the blower briefly. The ensuing maniacal wail caused windows several hundred yards away to be thrown open and the impression of a healthy boot in the car's rear end was distinctly felt.

The pushrod straight eight is a 306 cubic inch engine with a bore of $3\frac{3}{8}$ and stroke of $4\frac{1}{4}$ inches. The transmission provides three speeds forward plus overdrive, and second and high gear are synchronized. A foot-operated system lubricates the car. The car's ride is well controlled but extremely firm, the fine seats helping passenger comfort as much as the stiff suspension does. Purchased in Switzerland, the European restorer went to great pains to make this red and black beauty authentic. The body, chassis and engine came from two automobiles. When the work was completed, the machine was returned to Stuttgart, where Mercedes-Benz put on new body plates certifying the authentic entity of this beautiful cabriolet. Examining the superb workmanship, it is not hard to believe that these models were originally tagged at prices ranging from twelve to eighteen thousand depression dollars.

The 500K was followed by the "hotter" 540K and in 1938 by the 580K, but this car marks a turning point that was perhaps responsible for the successful policy of Mercedes-Benz today; that is, the combination of engineering, handling and fine performance wedded to the concept of a family touring automobile.

A 1936 British advertisement shows a Mercedes-Benz in a far-flung corner of the empire.

gine layout on left
e. Compare this well-
anized clutter with
clean compartment
the Hispano-Suiza.

ercharger side of the
cedes 306 cubic inch
ine.

Storage compartment under the hood showing new chassis and motor plates.

Speedometer on the 500K is calibrated to 200 kilometers per hour. Note grab strap.

Interior detail shows ash tray, grab strap and a door handle for the rear passenger. Each door has twin handles.

kish lines and a hood
f the length of the
are typical Merce-
-Benz trademarks.

graceful lines of
Mercedes belie its
prising weight of
0 pounds.

When folded, the top is too bulky for a graceful line.

Detail of faired-in trunk, a feature seen in many American automobiles of the period.

1934 DUESENBERG CONVERTIBLE SEDAN, MODEL J

Body by Murphy

A EUROPEAN writer once said, "There are automobiles of various qualities, and there is the Rolls-Royce." Most collectors and enthusiasts of great American cars would paraphrase that comment to apply to the Duesenberg. No other automobile made in this country has the magic of that name and reputation. No production car of its period ever delivered such performance, although it is unlikely that most owners demanded more than a fraction of what the big car could deliver. The great automobiles of 1934 were the 165 h.p. V-16 Cadillac, the 175 h.p. Pierce Arrow V-12 and the mighty Marmon V-12, rated at 200 h.p. In its standard version the Duesenberg delivers 265 h.p. and in the supercharged model that leaps to 320 h.p.

Few know that the obscure two-cylinder Mason of 1906 was Fred Duesenberg's first car. The Maytag Company bought out the Mason in 1910, and Fred Duesenberg and his brother August spent the next several years developing racing cars for the Indianapolis classic. In 1913 the brothers founded the Duesenberg Motors Company in Elizabeth, New Jersey. They were busy during World War I years producing the sixteen-cylinder Bugatti aircraft under license for the Allies. At the end of hostilities, the Duesenbergs sold their engine plant interests and went back to their unconventional four-cylinder racing engine. Versions of this engine appeared in the Biddle and Roamer cars. The Bugatti twin-eight had made a lasting impression on Fred Duesenberg, and he devoted his energies to producing a new straight eight. In 1920, a twin-engine special took the world's land speed title at 156 mph, and when this new engine powered the winner of the Grand Prix de France in 1921, the Duesenberg name was firmly established.

In the seventeen years of passenger car production Duesenberg made just two basic models. The Model A, a 95 h.p. straight eight, was produced at the

(*Opposite*) Front end of the "J." The company controlled the shape of radiator, hood and fenders to insure instant recognition of custom-bodied cars as Duesenbergs.

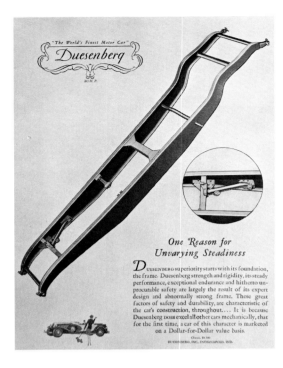

One Reason for
Unvarying Steadiness

DUESENBERG superiority starts with its foundation, the frame. Duesenberg strength and rigidity, its steady performance, exceptional endurance and hitherto unprocurable safety are largely the result of its expert design and abnormally strong frame. These great factors of safety and durability, are characteristic of the car's construction, throughout.... It is because Duesenberg does excel all other cars mechanically, that for the first time, a car of this character is marketed on a Dollar-for-Dollar value basis.

The advertisements for Duesenberg usually depicted a dashing sportsman with the casual copy line, "He drives a Duesenberg." This is one of the few ads in which engineering is discussed.

New Jersey plant in 1921. Production was soon shifted to the new Indianapolis plant, and some historians actually date Duesenberg production from this move. The Model A cost from $5,000 to $7,500 and had the first production car four-wheel hydraulic brakes. In five years fewer than a hundred cars were built, and this is the Duesenberg one never sees. How many survive is not known.

The president of Auburn, E. L. Cord, was quick to perceive that if his business and marketing ability were linked to the Duesenberg engineering genius, wealthy Americans might cease going to Europe for their luxury automobiles. In 1926, Duesenberg, Inc., was formed, with Fred Duesenberg moving into a new job as vice-president in charge of engineering and experimental work.

Cord handed him a blank check to produce the fastest, biggest and most powerful stock auto in the world. While this new machine was being developed, a car practically unknown today was made, the Model X. About twenty of these were completed, presumably to keep the name in the public eye until the Model J was finally ready in 1928.

The early "J" could be had in a wheelbase of 142½ inches and a super size at 153½ inches. The thirty-two valve straight eight displaced 420 cubic inches. The car was proved out at Indianapolis to deliver 116 mph. Its acceleration was fantastic, being capable of 90 mph in second gear. What made the "J" so outstanding was the excellence of steering, braking and ride. E. L. Cord had wisely decided to provide the chassis and leave the coach work to the leading American body builders—Murphy, Willoughby, Derham, Rollston, Brunn, Le Baron and others. They responded with stunning creations. Only a few La Grande bodies came directly from Duesenberg designs. When the last "J"

172

rolled out in 1937, some 470 automobiles had been made that would immortalize the Duesenberg name for car lovers the world over. It would take a chapter to enumerate the scores of features and refinements this ultimate motorcar possessed. Brake pressure could be adjusted from the dash, dials told when the acid in the battery was low. A frame that was 8½ inches deep, a mercury-filled vibration damper built into a crankshaft that was both statically and dynamically balanced were some of the costly features.

Costly it was, a basic chassis price of $8,500 was just the beginning. Although some builders quoted bodies for $3,500, the average complete "J" ran to over $16,500. Many of the "SJ's," with the ultimate in fur rugs, cocktail bars and duplicate instruments in the rear compartment, cost over $30,000.

Fred Duesenberg died in 1932 when his "SJ" left the road on a rainy day. Such was the impression left by these fewer than five hundred cars that twice attempts were made to revive the name. One in 1947 failed, a second undertaken in 1966 by Fred Duesenberg, Jr., only reached the stage of a completed prototype. This automobile was to have sold for $20,000. It might be pointed out that even in the rising market for classics, that sum will still buy an original Duesenberg of the "J" series.

Most of the external areas of the 265 h.p. Duesenberg eight are finished in enamel or chrome plating.

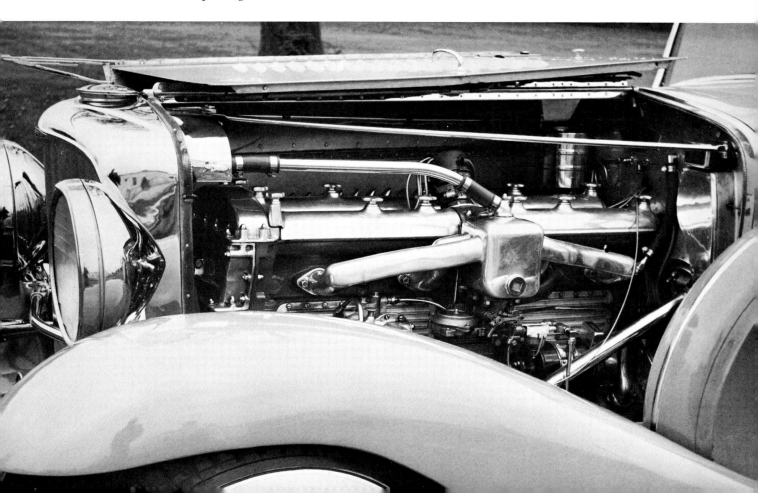

Engine-turned dash is recessed beneath the padded cowl. Flashing lights warned of low oil, battery acid, or fuel.

Scuff trim on the rear fender is a trademark of Murphy-bodied Duesenbergs.

ote the low center of
avity and wide tread
this high-perform-
ce sedan.

ofile of convertible
dan reveals its flawless
oportions. Note that
e hood is almost
actly half the car's
gth.

The side mounts are almost completely enclosed for trim appearance.

Murphy built more bodies for the "J" than any other coachmaker. The rear taillamp on this Duesenberg is a replica, as the restorer could not find one in sound condition.

1937 CORD
812 SC PHAETON

IT IS undoubtedly a compliment to the designer and builder of an automobile when that particular car is sought after, restored and treasured in great numbers by classic car enthusiasts. Packards, Lincolns and Cadillacs of the classic era certainly have received this compliment. What can be said, then, about three automobiles made under one man's direction, that not only are sought as classics but whose legendary fame has caused other builders to market near replicas in modern dress of all three? The three cars are, of course, Auburn, Cord and Duesenberg. The man who directed the corporation that marshaled the talent and imagination to produce these automotive greats was Erret Lobban Cord. In an engineering sense, today's plastic-bodied reduced-size models of the Cord and the forthcoming Auburn speedster are not related to their originals—nor was a huge, limited-production new Duesenberg a copy of an early Model J. The first two borrow the flawless style of the classic Auburn and Cord, while the last-mentioned borrows a name made legendary for superlative performance coupled with luxury. An earlier tribute paid to E. L. Cord and the car's designer, Gordon Buehrig, was the inclusion in 1952 of the Model 810 Cord in New York's Museum of Modern Art exhibition of outstanding coachwork in automobiles. To cite a fifteen-year-old design as the finest current example was to indicate how timeless Buehrig's concept was.

By astute judgment of the talents of people and of the potential of a sick company, E. L. Cord had built a corporation of great automotive ability by 1930. In 1924, he had acquired the moribund Auburn company, which was founded in 1900. He acquired the Duesenberg Motors Company in 1927, knowing the slow sales of its car were no reflection on the genius of Fred and August Duesenberg. In 1929 he added the Lycoming Aircraft interest and called the package the Cord Corporation.

While the Model J was building the company a fine reputation, Cord introduced the car bearing his name in 1929. The Lycoming straight-eight-powered L-29 was unveiled just two months before the stock market crash, however, and a dwindling market, plus transmission troubles of the front-wheel-drive car, resulted in poor sales. Total units produced were under 4,500.

179

(*Opposite*) Detail of the external exhaust pipes.

The Cord was advertised as a performance car that was master of every other car on the road.

By 1935, Cord determined to attempt another front-drive car in the upper-middle price range. Actual sketches for a "baby" Duesenberg that Buehrig had drawn in 1933 were examined, and that project having been shelved, it was decided to use the basic styling around a V-8 Lycoming engine. The original chassis designed by August Duesenberg was reworked for front drive and here began perhaps the only major error in judgment in the whole 810 and 812 program. A Herculean effort was made to get the new car ready for the New York Automobile Show of 1935. At the time it was thought that by over-time factory shifts, one hundred cars could be hand-assembled (the minimum amount required to classify a car as in production) and the show deadline met. Complications in the front-drive transmission arose and the Cord was in the embarrassing position of being the style hit of the show although unavailable for delivery or even large-scale demonstration. A well-engineered concept throughout, normal delays typical of such a novel arrangement of engine and transmission were exaggerated by rival salesmen. It was easy to take a Cord out on the road and to chip gears by attempting fast gear changes. The short, finger-operated lever changed gears by vacuum, magnetically selected. It was slow, and early models were not equipped with an interlock to prevent accidentally shifting into an incorrect gear. All this plus some overheating prob-

180

lems obscured the fact that the performance of the car was little short of sensational. The supercharged 812 reached 0-60 in 13.2 seconds and had a top speed variously listed as from 102 to 110 mph.

John Longo spotted this 812 phaeton in 1958 in a lot on Long Island next to some rental garages. The car was in poor condition and bore no plates. Despite several attempts, he was unable to find the owner. While doing business in the same block two years later, he casually inquired about the Cord that had been there two years before and was given its owner's address. This time he was successful and acquired the car. Although in poor to fair condition, it had the advantage of being a late model with the shift interlock and several other minor changes incorporated. The major fault was a thoroughly damaged transmission, including the case. Work ceased until this problem was solved by locating a man in Manhattan who owned two derelict Cord sedans and a pile of parts. One car had a perfect transmission, and as a mere overhaul cost $350 at the time, Mr. Longo cheerfully paid $300 for the whole package.

Restoration was finally finished, including interior, paint, tires and engine overhaul. Several meets later Mr. Longo concluded that restoration was a relative term and that compared to the other Cords he had seen, his could be better. This time, he tore the car down to the frame. Not a washer that could be removed was left on, every unit was disassembled and the sand blasting began. The engine came out, and Mr. Longo personally performed a re-bore, reground the crankshaft and installed new valves and pistons. Lycoming parts were found to be easily available. Parts for the Switzer-Cummins supercharger were impossible to find, and fortunately none was needed for a successful overhaul. Since this time the ACD Club has been able to encourage a parts maker to prepare some of the scarce molding trim and other parts needed for Cord restoration.

When the car was finished after two years of work, three weeks of road tests were made before "closing up" the Cord for the final painting. Several adjustments had to be made to the electrical circuits and linkage of the vacuum shift. In three thousand miles of driving during the next several months no difficulties were experienced.

The automobile has won one major award after another for its restorer and its new owner, Harold Houser. A first place in the Grand Classic at Morristown, New Jersey, in 1965, a first at Hershey, Pennsylvania, in 1965 and a best in show at the 1966 National Auburn, Cord, Duesenberg Club meet are a few of the honors accorded this beautiful 812 phaeton.

181

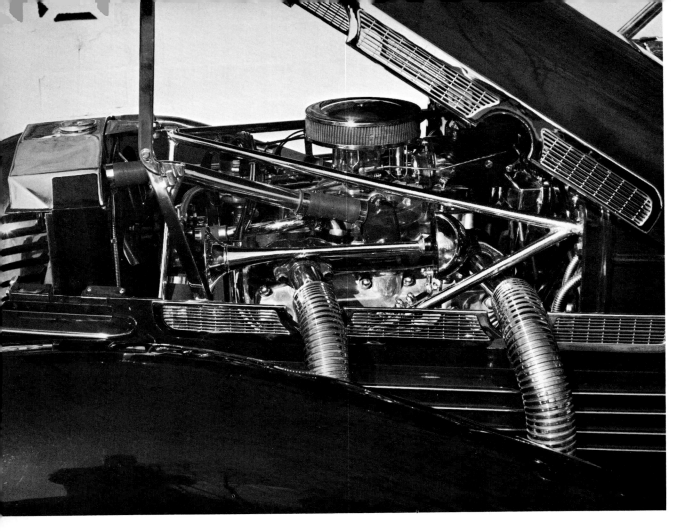

The Lycoming V-8, displacing 288 cubic inches with a bore and stroke of 3½ x 3¾ inches. With super charger, output was raised to 170 h.p. at 4,250 r.p.m.

Transmission of the forward drive Cord 812 was between the radiator and grill.

Easily the most dazzling dash ever mounted on an American production car. Large toggle switches were for lights, gas and choke. Clock had a sweep second hand; a large tachometer was next to the speedometer. Small keg-shaped fixture on steering column is the pre-selector vacuum-gear shift.

Beautiful interior of the five-passenger Cord phaeton.

Headlamps are elevated to operating position by a crank at either side of dash. The owner's manual requests drivers to keep headlights closed in daylight "to add immeasurably to the beauty of the new Cord."

A view from above shows the impressive length of the hood. This Cord phaeton is an authentic deep maroon.

The bumper is a distinctive feature of the 1937 Cord.

Cord lines are pleasing even with the top up.

From a low angle, the Continental nose is virtually identical with the Zephyr; the main grille comes from Zephyr factory parts bins.

1941 LINCOLN
CONTINENTAL COUPE

MOST OF the great cars of the classic era bear the stamp of one brilliant engineer or designer. The Gordon Buehrig 812 Cord, Ettore Bugatti's Royale and the superlative Hispano-Suiza of Marc Birkigt were cars whose design was strongly dominated by one personality. In the case of the Continental, all the more credit seems due Edsel Ford (and the Ford design staff, led by Eugene T. Gregorie, who fulfilled Ford's wishes) for his achievement. Ford simply wanted a one-of-a-kind version of the Lincoln-Zephyr for his personal use. What resulted, though it bore a family resemblance to the Zephyr line, and used much of its sheet metal and power plant, was the creation of a stunning new aristocrat. The Continental achieved its elegance by virtue of graceful line, faultless proportion and the courage to leave huge masses of sheet metal clean and unadorned. Mr. Ford insisted on retaining the spare wheel in an exposed well so the rear end had a dash lacking in the wind tunnel tail of the Zephyr. This Continental coupe is an interesting example of the envelope principle in industrial design: that is, the housing of each unit—the wheels, the engine room, the passenger compartment and the trunk—in a harmonious covering that doesn't distort each shape or misrepresent its purpose.

Using Zephyr parts, the graceful lines were produced by adding to the length of the hood and the front fenders. Twelve inches were added to the prototype, but this was reduced to eight inches in the second and third cars made for Edsel Ford's two sons. The doors of the prototype, a convertible, were lowered by cutting the panels horizontally and removing a four-inch strip. When the hand-built car was finished, it was lower, longer and wider than any Lincoln Zephyr, and it made that machine look high-roofed and stubby by comparison. This first Continental, still sporting a Zephyr nameplate on its nose, was delivered to Edsel Ford vacationing in Florida, and in a matter of months the legend was born.

With several hundred orders in hand, only twenty-five Continentals could be produced in 1939. With the sketchiest of assembly lines and using some wooden dies sheathed in metal to avoid the delay and cost of making special steel dies, four hundred or so were delivered the following year. In 1941, Mr.

187

NEXT BEST THING TO FLYING

Lincoln Zephyr V-12

The 1937 Lincoln-Zephyr was the predecessor of the Continental.

Bailey's coupe was one of twelve hundred Continentals produced. This machine listed at $2,727 in 1941, which was relatively cheap then for a luxury automobile. Despite the success of the face-lifted versions that were made between 1946 and 1948, the limited sales potential of a car still made largely by hand forced a decision to end its run after a total of 5,324 Continentals. This figure, covering six model years, is equaled every month by the current edition of the Lincoln Continental.

The Model H V-12 engine, standard for the Zephyr, powered the Continental, and was dressed up with aluminum cylinder heads secured by acorn nuts. This engine developed a modest 120 h.p. at 3,600 r.p.m. and according to today's Continental enthusiasts is a far better engine than prewar mechanics gave it credit for.

The value of a one-marque club cannot be overestimated in the case of the Continental. The Lincoln Continental Owners' Club is the clearing house for information on maintenance and repair of this last of America's "twelves." Members frequently acquire stocks of Continental and Zephyr parts from dealers and make them available to other Continental enthusiasts.

A remarkable point of this coupe, owned by Jackson Bailey, is that it took Best of Show Award at the Classic Car Club meet in Buck Hill Falls, Pennsylvania, in 1966, wearing the original upholstery inside and the original thirteen-coat factory-baked enamel paint outside. This is a tribute to the devoted care given it over a twenty-five year period by Mr. Bailey and the car's one previous owner. Minor replating and a complete rebuild on the engine to exact factory-new condition was the extent of restoration necessary. This jet-black beauty still causes heads to turn when it purrs along Long Island roads, and after twenty-five years that tribute alone would satisfy Edsel Ford.

188

Sparkling engine room houses a completely rebuilt Lincoln V-12.

Driver's view shows the really beautiful steering wheel and the early use of plastic in dash controls. The wood grain decal over the steel dash is convincing. Late model Mercury decals have been used in Continental restoration.

Note the slight upsweep in the lower fender and the rocker panel trim. The extremely thin line of the roof pillar leads many to consider the Continental the first hardtop, though it is a true coupe.

The squared-off and broader roof line sets the Continental apart from the Zephyr.

Had Edsel Ford yielded to his design staff, the spare wheel would have been stored inside the trunk. The arrangement shown gives the Lincoln Continental much of its distinction.

6. THE SPECIAL-INTEREST AUTOMOBILE

IF a vehicle is not an accepted classic and is too recent a vintage to be considered antique, it is usually referred to as a special-interest car. Unfortunately, this all too frequently includes automobiles whose sole claim to fame is that by some quirk of climate (or a heated garage) they have merely survived several decades. Without being pedantic, if a car merits the description "special interest," it should be distinguished either by unusual body style, an engineering innovation or some other marked difference from the routine production of its day. A 1937 Lincoln Zephyr would qualify easily by virtue of its revolutionary wind tunnel streamlining and V-12 engine, an American Bantam of 1939 by virtue of its diminutive size, and the 1934 Chrysler Airflow because of a host of engineering features that it introduced.

The term, however, seems to be used more in connection with the special interest each collector has in his particular car, and it seems unlikely any standard tests can be applied successfully to this category. Then again, why should there be? If one group is enthusiastic about Kaiser products and if a club is formed to preserve Edsels, who would deny them their fun? The great virtue of special-interest cars is that there are enough to go around for everybody. They include automobiles that are antiques as well, such as the Nash, Buick, Star, LaFayette and Rockne. Many mint restorations of certain models, a 1929 Studebaker President Roadster or a 1932 Nash Cabriolet, rival many classics in appearance and will be increasingly sought after as classics grow scarcer. Every reader will have his own preferences, but for a starting point here are some nominations for special-interest cars of merit. These cars will usually descend in cost from the older models to the recent choices.

Let's start with some recent automobiles whose popularity with collectors

(*Opposite*) The 1935 Ford phaeton.

This Naugatuck Chemical advertisement featured the Kaiser-Darrin sports car. Fewer than 400 were made, and today they cost almost as much as when new.

The New Yorker magazine ran this Bantam advertisement in 1930. The Bantams are interesting and rare.

The 1953 Caribbean, which cost over $5,000, is thought by many to be the finest-looking of the last Packards.

The coupe Raymond Loewy designed for Studebaker in 1953 was widely praised for its beautiful lines.

seems assured. A personal favorite, and undoubtedly the most inexpensive automobile mentioned in this volume, is the graceful sports coupe or hardtop Raymond Loewy designed for the 1953 and 1954 Studebaker line. This car was available as the six-cylinder Champion or V-8 Commander. In 1954 quality control was improved over the first model year and larger brakes were fitted. In the eight-cylinder version equipped with standard shift and overdrive, it was an excellent road car. At the present time in the New York area $30 to $100 will buy a solid easily restorable edition of this model. Its simple lines and basic good design are proved by the fact that until the mid-sixties, Studebaker was able to face-lift this car in several versions, including the Packard Hawk and the Gran Turismo.

Packard's last efforts to stay alive as a quality car before its merger with Studebaker in 1957 produced several fine machines, notably the Caribbean convertibles from 1953 through 1956. These cars bridged the change from the mighty nine-bearing straight eight to the modern V-8 engine. Beside the striking convertibles in 1955 to 1956, a Model 400 hardtop was notable.

Other postwar cars that should be considered are:

Ford Thunderbird, 1955 through 1957
Ford Sportsman convertible, 1947
Studebaker Starlight coupe, 1947
Buick Skylark convertible, 1953
Kaiser-Frazer Virginian hardtop sedan, 1949
Kaiser-Darrin Fiberglas sports car, 1953
Chrysler Town and Country convertible, 1947 through 1949
Lincoln Cosmopolitan Fastback sedan, 1949 and 1950
Willys Jeepster, 1949 and 1950

1954 Kaiser Special. The Manhattan model of the same year featured supercharger and the same attractive front end.

Some prewar cars of note:

Hupp Skylark, 1939-1940
Lincoln Zephyr, particularly the touring sedan, 1937 through 1941
Buick touring sedan and roadster, Century and Roadmaster models, 1937 and 1938
Chrysler and DeSoto Airflow, 1934 through 1936
Model A Ford, 1927 through 1932

Certain models of Buicks, Hudsons, Nashs and Studebakers in the 1929 through 1934 period are surprisingly attractive. Touring sedans and roadsters are first choice but scarce. Some two-door sedans and broughams with wire-wheel side mounts gleaming and a nickel-trimmed trunk on the rack are quite striking. This is one area of the old-car hobby where $500 may still buy a worthwhile vehicle. Because of uncertain value considerations, beware of cars requiring major restoration at great expense. A rising market in classics seems certain, but it is impossible to predict what special-interest car may catch on and be sought after in future years.

This is the area of the old-car hobby where the enthusiast of limited means may still acquire a worthwhile vehicle at moderate cost that will provide as much family fun (and restoration challenge) as many aristocratic classics.

An advertising picture of an ill-fated but fascinating special interest car, the Chrysler Airflow eight.

(*Opposite*) 1957 Thunderbird, with porthole windows in its removable hard top.

1929 FORD, MODEL A STATION WAGON

TO appreciate the detailed story behind the introduction of the Model A in 1928, it is necessary to understand how Henry Ford ran his empire on the River Rouge. In this day and age no manufacturer would take the risk of introducing a new car without motivation research, market research, and scores of conferences to explore every angle of the proposed new vehicle. Henry Ford was a man of intuitive judgments. His major decisions about the fantastically successful Model T were based solely on his own judgment, frequently in the face of opposition from key aides. While millions were riding in comfortable cars with four-wheel brakes and hydraulic shock absorbers in the late twenties, Ford was still grinding out the car made for the roads of fifteen years before. Falling sales did not budge him. He blamed the slump on a complacent sales force. In 1927 the unthinkable happened and Chevrolet outsold Ford for the first time since they had challenged each other in 1916.

Edsel Ford, nominally president of the company, was striving to bring out a new model. His father was agreeable, providing his beloved planetary transmission was retained. Ford Sr. asked his engineering staff to devise a way of making the planetary gear shifts automatic. Had the torque converter principle been examined more closely at this time, another "first" might have been added to Ford's list. While various departments worked on parts of what would be the Model A, the production lines were halted and no cars were made for nine months. It is said that the Model A came forth in eight months, but Charles Sorensen, production head for Ford, stated that after Henry made up his mind, it took just ninety days. It is startling that the new car did offer so many advanced features.

After fifteen million Model Ts wearing mortuary black, it seemed incredible to be offered Mulberry Maroon, Cigarette Cream and Andalusite Blue. The "A" drew crowds to admire its Houdaille shock absorbers, its Triplex safety glass windshield and its 200 cubic inch four-cylinder engine. In general appearance it was close to the road, had a modern, attractive interior and seemed to belong to the current scene. The public looked and ordered. In 1928,

199

(*Opposite*) At $650, this Ford station wagon was considerably more expensive than the phaeton "A."

THE FUN OF OLD CARS

633,594 were sold. Sales hit 1,507,132 in 1929. Sales in 1930 were down, and in the soup-kitchen days of 1931 dropped below the first model year of 1928. Even the best $500 car in America couldn't be sold in a depression-gripped land. Total production of the Model A between 1928 and 1932 was almost five million. It is estimated that 300,000 still exist, in condition ranging from pampered prize winners to battered hulks serving farmers yet in the backwoods.

The 1929 station wagon illustrated is a fairly rare model. Less than ten percent of all "A" production cars were fitted with station wagon bodies. Also, 1929 was the last year for nickel plating on headlamps and radiator grill. Easier-to-maintain chrome was used from 1930 on.

The rock maple body of this wagon is entirely original. Side curtains were replaced after accurate patterns were obtained from an original set. The extraordinary condition of the wood is partly due to the vehicle's low original mileage. The first owner ran it just 36,000 miles from 1929 until 1948, garaging it after every trip. When he retired the wagon in 1948, he contacted the local Model A club to see if anyone cared to buy it. William Evans acquired it and restored it from the frame up. The chassis was sandblasted and every inch of metal cleaned, including the springs which were disassembled. Only the side mirror was missing from the Ford. Restoration was to a standard of perfection that won a first place at Hershey, Pennsylvania, in the Junior Division of the Antique Automobile Club of America as well as a National first place in the Model A Ford Club meet.

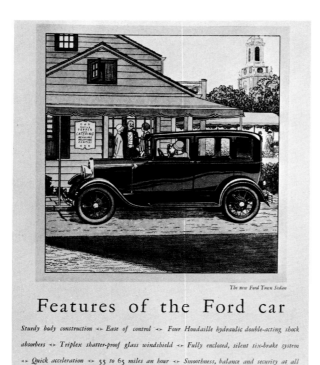

The new Ford Town Sedan

Features of the Ford car

Sturdy body construction ‹› *Ease of control* ‹› *Four Houdaille hydraulic double-acting shock absorbers* ‹› *Triplex shatter-proof glass windshield* ‹› *Fully enclosed, silent six-brake system* ‹› *Quick acceleration* ‹› *55 to 65 miles an hour* ‹› *Smoothness, balance and security at all speeds* ‹› *Vibration-absorbing engine support* ‹› *Choice of colors* ‹› *Tilting beam headlamps* ‹› *Theft-proof ignition lock* ‹› *Reliability* ‹› *Economy* ‹› *Long life*

Hearst's International-Cosmopolitan for August 1929

For the first time a Ford advertisement considered style and comfort as selling points for the new "A."

The 40 h.p. four-cylinder engine. The finned manifold could be fitted with a shell adapting it for duty as a heater.

The dash of the "A" is as functional as that of the later-day
jeep.

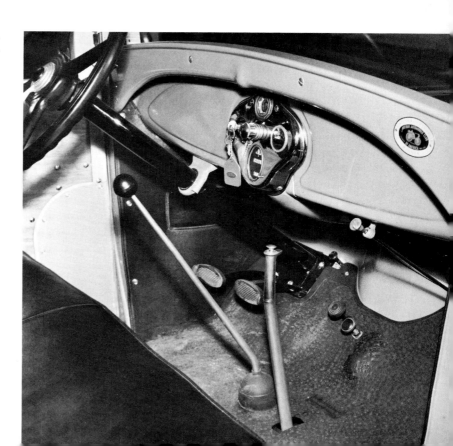

The interior was strictly functional. Note the angle-iron corners, which ensure a rigid body.

Graceful door handles relieve the stark lines of the station wagon.

Note the large tailgate.

Side view shows the pleasing proportions of the Murray-built body.

The chrome wheel discs on this Ford were an optional accessory.

1935 FORD PHAETON, MODEL 750

ALTHOUGH the Model A had been a successful stopgap, Edsel and Henry Ford knew that a new and advanced automobile was needed to blunt the inroads into the Ford market that the fine Chevrolet six was making. Since 1929 the Chevy was always 10 or 15 h.p. ahead of the Model A, and its six was a smooth, quiet engine.

In 1932, Ford's answer was ready in a brilliant new engine, a V-8 of 65 h.p. The engine was quickly put into a slightly revised "A" and announced as the "B" series. In a few years the stylists caught up with the engine, and the 1934 through 1936 models were beautiful cars.

The V-8 that could be produced cheaply enough for a low-cost car was largely due to factory techniques that were developed under "Cast-iron Charlie" Sorensen, production chief for Ford. The cylinder blocks, crankcase and exhaust passages were cast in a single unit. A mechanized line brought molds to an iron-pouring line at a rate of one hundred an hour. It was an unprecedented operation, since both lines were moving continuously even during the pouring of the molten metal. The next step was to develop and substitute cast steel crankshafts for the more expensive forgings. Stronger and lighter steel pistons were the final casting achievement in the V-8 development story.

Most sought after today by collectors are the roadsters and phaetons. Mr. Snowden located his phaeton in California. It had been used for many years as a delivery car for the *Los Angeles Times*. The engine had been rebuilt by its owner, but the rest of the car was quite decrepit. Robert Snowden decided to buy the car and to drive it home. This 3,000-mile epic began in February, and by the time the new owner had reached Phoenix, he was bucking blizzards. A detour south to El Paso to avoid the snow followed, with Mr. Snowden maintaining a twelve-hour, five-hundred-mile-a-day pace. At one point the bitter cold forced him to fabricate a cardboard shelter out of a large carton wedged in the front seat of the open car. The only major halt was an enforced overnight stop to repair a throwout bearing in the clutch, which required pulling

205

the engine. Followed by another savage blizzard, Mr. Snowden kept one jump ahead by driving the final 850 miles in one stretch.

During the restoration of this phaeton, a trip was made to President Franklin Roosevelt's home in Hyde Park. Here careful measurements were taken from the top of F.D.R.'s Ford phaeton. This well-preserved favorite of the late President had hand controls and its top was authentic in cut and fit. Robert Snowden rebuilt the brakes, had trim replated and a new leather interior installed in his car. The columns of *Hemmings Motor News* and local old-car flea markets supplied the parts required.

The phaeton is capable of maintaining a steady cruising speed of 50 mph and has taken the Snowdens on many tours. This is a Ford family, the 1935 V-8 being flanked in the family garage by a well-restored Model T and a mint 1955 Thunderbird.

"Charles Sorensen's triumph," the one-piece unit 85 h.p. V-8 that won many hill-climbing events for Ford drivers.

Wind wings are among the most prized of the original accessories. These are original, but duplicates are being manufactured today for several automobiles of the past.

One of the twin horns. These were a Ford trademark on the 1935 models.

The rear had unusually graceful lines. The lack of a trunk was remedied by a storage locker behind the rear seat.

In profile, the Ford looks longer than its 112 inch wheelbase. The vehicle weighs 2,667 pounds.

1937 BUICK ROADMASTER
CONVERTIBLE SEDAN,
MODEL 80C

DAVID DUNBAR BUICK is readily identified as one of the early automobile pioneers. His other notable contribution to American progress, and some might say the greater, was to bring forth the glittering all-white American bathroom. A Detroit plumber with an inventive mind, he developed a method to successfully porcelainize iron. This revolutionized the manufacture of bath fixtures and made Buick wealthy. He soon turned his inquiring mind to automobile design, and the fledgling Buick Motor Company of Detroit produced a dozen or so two-cylinder cars in 1903. He sold out his interest that same year to W. C. Durant. Five years later the General Motors empire was created when Durant added Oakland and Oldsmobile to the Buick cornerstone. With talent like Charles Nash, Louis Chevrolet and Walter P. Chrysler contributing their efforts, Buick was soon one of the most stable companies. Production was up to 10,000 cars a year by 1909.

In 1914, Buick changed from four to six cylinders. At times they had experimented with eights, twelves, and even a V-6. In 1931 they went up to eight cylinders to claim a place within the middle price range of powerful cars. Twenty-five models, in four series of valve-in-head eights, ranged in price from less than $1,000 to slightly over $2,000.

Mechanically, Buick was one of the finer cars produced in the late twenties and early thirties. It was styled for the solid, conservative, well-to-do American family. No effort was made to make it an avant-garde style leader as was done with the LaSalle.

By 1937, the General Motors line was characterized by exceptionally clean lines, with the convertibles being notably attractive. At Buick, fewer than a thousand convertible sedans were built on the 131 inch Roadmaster chassis. The "oil-cushioned" straight eight produced 130 h.p. at 3,400 r.p.m., having a bore and stroke of $3\frac{7}{16}$ x $4\frac{5}{16}$.

This Buick came to the attention of Don Gilbert and John Lindhardt when a telephone repairman casually mentioned seeing a large dusty convertible

211

(*Opposite*) Close-set headlights were a feature of General Motors cars of the late thirties.

with 1953 plates standing in a customer's garage. The lead was followed up, and the owner let Mr. Lindhardt inspect the car. Her late husband had owned and babied the 1937 Buick, and she had kept it for sentimental reasons. Only when she was convinced that a serious restoration was intended did she agree to sell the machine. It had not been moved for twelve years and the brakes had literally frozen. Jacking up the car and working the wheels back and forth soon released them. The clutch had seized up and had to be freed.

A new grill was found in the corner of a dusty window at an old established automobile parts store. The car has been re-lacquered in the deep green Buick favored that year and new Denman tires have been mounted. Authentic fender flaps as well as some chrome trim were found at the annual Hershey flea market. The engine required little work other than to rebuild the carburetor. The bumpers, which are slightly different for this Roadmaster from the standard Buick line, will require replating. The interior requires re-upholstery to complete the restoration, and that might well be the most expensive item, as a re-do in Naugahyde could run to $500.

Because of its attractive appearance, its sprightly performance lending itself to family touring and its limited production, this Buick is an exceptionally fine example of a distinctive special-interest car.

The valve-in-head eight develops 130 h.p. at 3,400 r.p.m.

Lines that seemed stodgy on the closed sedan become elegant on the convertible, particularly with the sunken side-mounted spares.

1949 CHRYSLER
TOWN AND COUNTRY
CONVERTIBLE

WALTER P. CHRYSLER was another of the early pioneers who came out of the most demanding engineering classrooms of his day, the locomotive shop. Having risen to works manager at American Locomotive at the age of thirty-six, he turned to the rapidly expanding automobile industry and joined Buick in 1911 as head of that unit of General Motors. In 1920, after he had upped Buick's production tenfold, he startled the automotive world by resigning his presidency of a division that had just turned an annual profit of almost fifty million dollars to plunge into the red ink at Willys-Overland. He reduced that company's debt by forty million in a few years and had created a strong demand for the Overland car. His reputation as a wizard with failing automobile makers was established, and the next call for help he answered led to the creation of the first Chrysler automobile. He purchased Maxwell-Chalmers when a debt of thirty million dollars was crippling that company's operations. He launched the first car bearing his name, the Model B Chrysler Six, at the National Auto Show in 1924. It looked like a Maxwell, but its new engine that could cruise at seventy, four-wheel hydraulic brakes and a steel body by Fisher created a sensation. The Chase Corporation lent Chrysler fifty million dollars and soon 100,000 Model B's were delivered.

Chrysler thrived in the next several years. The standard production cars sold well and performed exceptionally well but the basic factory body design made few heads turn. The light sixes seemed to be considered the bread-and-butter line requiring no frills, but fortunately Chrysler felt differently about his big sixes and powerful eights. The E-80, a 92 h.p. six, had been made since 1926 on several chassis, including one of 133 inches. Various models of the Imperial were successful in European races, a Chrysler taking second in the Belgian Grand Prix of 1928.

Chrysler hit his stride with the production of the C G Imperial Custom Eight in 1930. In every respect a great classic, its 384 cubic inch engine devel-

215

(*Opposite*) From the front, the Town and Country
resembles the regular line of Chryslers.

A massive, heavily sculptured effect was favored by Chrysler stylists, as this dash indicates.

oped 125 h.p. and was marred only by a cranky four-speed transmission. The ever-reliable three-speed Chrysler unit was finally substituted in 1934, but not until the big Imperial's reputation had suffered somewhat. In 1932 the model C L was introduced on a 145 inch wheelbase, virtually the same size vehicle as the Duesenberg and Hispano-Suiza. The prestige body builders looked at the sweeping hood and fenders and hastened to their drawing boards. Locke, Brewster, Murphy, Dietrich, Rollston, Brunn and Le Baron all made bodies for the Chrysler Imperial and the Crown Imperial.

In 1934, Chrysler introduced a new line of cars called the Chrysler Airflow. In one of their first advertisements Chrysler stated that

> Pioneers are apt to be people who are sure of themselves . . . go their own way . . . make decisions with independence.

Although this is admirable, in the automobile business it can also be fatal. The revolutionary concepts of suspension, weight distribution, and streamlining just did not add up to an attractive automobile. Three eights and a six were in the line, with a wheelbase choice ranging from 118 to 146 inches. One item

216

Distinctive taillights are set in fender sides. Note the sweep of the wrap-around rear bumper.

that must have hurt sales was that the cheapest eight at $1,245 looked substantially like the Custom Imperial Sedan Limousine at $5,145. The automobile was reputed to be unstable due to the heavier weight of the front end, and its floating ride was said to be at the price of precise handling. The fine engine performance of both six and eight could not offset the body styling, and when it was phased out in 1937, fewer than 30,000 units of all models had been sold. It is certainly one of the worthier special-interest cars around today, and any model on the 137 or 146 inch wheelbase is worth acquiring. Both the six and eight were offered as convertibles, and these are considerably more attractive than the sedans.

In the intervening years, before the massive Town and Country models were introduced in 1947, few Chryslers of startling distinction appeared. Derham and Le Baron did some bodies for Chryslers of the late thirties but only the 1939, 1941 Newport Le Baron phaetons are really striking.

When the long hood required by the straight eights of this Town and Country series disappeared in 1950 with the advent of the V-8, the day of long graceful line in body style seemed over.

The wood body panels of the Town and Country require periodic applications of varnish.

The long hood was a Chrysler feature until the straight eight was replaced by the shorter V-8 in 1950.

The fine proportions of the Town and Country were enhanced by horizontal trim.

AUTOMOBILE CLUBS

Most of the larger automobile clubs publish monthly bulletins, which keep members abreast of club activities and carry classified advertisements. Club membership dues, which usually range from five to ten dollars a year, include subscriptions to the bulletins and to the attractive magazines published by the large clubs. These publications carry news of tours and meets as well as classified advertising for cars and car parts.

The Council of Historic Automotive Societies at Cicero, New York, publishes a one dollar directory listing seventy American "one-make" clubs and many foreign automobile clubs.

A selected list of automobile clubs:

The Antique Automobile Club of America, Inc., West Derry Rd., Hershey, Pennsylvania 17033

Auburn Cord Duesenberg Owners Club, Box 147, Milpitas, California 95035

Big Seven Restorers Club, Box 447, Downey, California 96418

The Classic Car Club of America, 114 Liberty Street, New York, New York 10006

The Horseless Carriage Club of America, 9031 E. Florence Avenue, Downey, California

Lincoln Continental Owner's Club, National Headquarters, 28 Harmony Lane, Westbury, New York.

Model A Ford Club of America, P.O. Box 2564, Pomona, California 91766

Model A Restorers Club, P.O. Box 1930A, Dearborn, Michigan 48121

Packard Automobile Classics, Inc., P.O. Box 2808, Oakland, California 96418

Packard International Motor Car Club, P.O. Box 1347, Costa Mesa, California

Pierce Arrow Society, Inc., 142 Vaser Street, Rochester, New York, 14607

The Steam Automobile Club of America, Inc., 1937 E. 71st Street, Chicago 40, Illinois

The Studebaker Driver's Club, Inc., 30 Chicago Avenue, Bellmore, Long Island, New York 11710

The Veteran Motor Car Club of America, 15 Newton Street, Brookline, Massachusetts 02146

Vintage Chevrolet Club of America, Elmer Ryan, 9214 Higdale St., Bellflower, California

AUTOMOBILE MUSEUMS

It is advisable to determine the schedule of visiting hours and days open before traveling to any museum. This selection of museums is listed according to geographical location, east to west.

VMCCA Antique Auto Museum, Larz Anderson Park, Brookline, Massachusetts 02146

Long Island Automotive Museum, Southampton, Long Island, New York

The Carriage House, Stony Brook, Long Island, New York (Superb collection of pre-automotive era carriages)

Smithsonian Institution, Transportation Division, Washington, D.C.

Gene Zimmerman's Antique Car Museum, Harrisburg, Pennsylvania

Boyertown Auto Body Works Collection, Boyertown, Pennsylvania

Bellm Cars and Music of Yesterday, 5500 North Tamiami Trail, Sarasota, Florida

Museum of Speed, P.O. Box 4157 Daytona Beach, Florida 32021

Elliot Museum of Vehicular Evolution, Hutchinson Island, Stuart, Florida

Frederick C. Crawford Auto-Aviation Museum of the Western Reserve Historical Society, 10825 East Boulevard, Cleveland, Ohio 44106

Henry Ford Museum & Greenfield Village, Dearborn, Michigan

Brooks Stevens Automotive Museum, Route 141, Mequon, Wisconsin

Museum of Science and Industry, Chicago, Illinois

The Museum of Automobiles, Winthrop Rockefeller Collection, Petit Jean Mountain, Arkansas

Harold Warp's Pioneer Village, Minden, Nebraska 68959

Harrah's Auto Collection, Reno, Nevada

Briggs Cunningham Automotive Museum, 250 Baker Street, Costa Mesa, California

AUTOMOTIVE LIBRARIES

Information on old automobiles can be obtained from these libraries. Charges vary but are usually based on an hourly rate for the librarian's time and the cost of the necessary photostats. The major automotive libraries are:

Automotive History Collection, The Detroit Public Library, 5201 Woodward Avenue, Detroit, Michigan

Frederick Crawford Auto-Aviation Museum, Western Reserve Historical Society, 10825 Ead Boulevard, Cleveland, Ohio 44106. Mrs. Ruth F. Sommerlad, Director

The Ford Archives, Henry Ford Museum, Dearborn, Michigan

Long Island Automotive Research, Meadow Spring, Glen Cove, New York

Thomas McKean Collection of the Automobile, The Free Library of Philadelphia, Logan Square, Philadelphia, Pennsylvania

SELECTED BIBLIOGRAPHY

On Automobiles

Bentley, W. O. *The Cars in My Life*. New York: Macmillan Company, 1963.

Bergere, Thea and Richard. *Automobiles of Yesteryear*. New York: Dodd, Mead & Company, 1962.

Bird, Anthony. *The Motor Car: 1765–1914*. London: Batsford, 1960.

Borgeson, Griffith, and Jaderquist, Eugene. *Sports and Classic Cars*. New York: Prentice-Hall, 1955.

Buckley, J. R. *Cars of the Connoisseur*. New York: Macmillan Company, 1962.

Clutton, C., Bird, Paul, and Harding, Anthony. *The Vintage Motor Car*. Pocketbook. London: Batsford, 1961.

Clymer Floyd. *Those Wonderful Old Automobiles*. New York: Crown Publishers, 1953.

SELECTED BIBLIOGRAPHY

Doyle, George R. *The World's Automobiles.* California: Floyd Clymer Publications, 1962.

Helck, Peter. *The Checkered Flag.* New York: Charles Scribner's Sons, 1961.

Hough, Richard, and Frostick, Michael. *A History of the World's Classic Cars.* New York: Harper & Row, 1963.

Hough, Richard, Ed. *Motor Car Lover's Companion.* New York: Harper & Row, 1965.

Markmann, Charles Lam, and Sherwin, Mark. *The Book of Sport Cars.* New York: J. P. Putnam's Sons, 1959.

Maxim, Hiram P. *Horseless Carriage Days.* New York: Harper & Brothers, 1937.

Purdy, Ken W. *The Kings of the Road.* Boston; Little, Brown & Company, 1953.

Purdy, Ken W. *Motorcars of the Golden Past.* Photographs by Tom Burnside. Boston: Atlantic-Little, Brown & Company, 1966.

Rae, John B. *The American Automobile.* Chicago, Ill.: The University of Chicago Press, 1966.

Scott-Moncrieff, David. *Classic Cars: 1930–1940.* Cambridge, Mass.: Robert Bentley, Inc., 1963.

Scott-Moncrieff, David. *Veteran and Edwardian Cars.* London: Batsford, 1961.

Sheel, J. D. *Cars of the World in Color.* New York: E. P. Dutton, 1963.

Stein, Ralph. *The Treasury of the Automobile.* New York: Ridge-Golden Press, 1961.

On Automobile Restoration

Henry, Leslie R. *Model T Ford Restoration Handbook.* Los Angeles, California: Floyd Clymer Publications, 1966.

Hopper, George E. *Model A Ford Restoration Handbook.* Los Angeles, California: Floyd Clymer Publications, 1966.

How To Restore Antique and Classic Cars. Chicago, Illinois: Popular Mechanics Press, 1954.

Morgan, Brian and Wheatley, Richard C. *The Restoration of Antique and Classic Cars.* Cambridge, Massachusetts: Robert Bentley, Inc., 1964.

Periodicals

Hobby publications, which range from classified advertisement pamphlets to the slick paper magazines of the major clubs, list such specialized services as plating shops, wooden and wire wheel rebuilders, and cut and fit upholstery services. Automobile parts, of course, are also advertised.

A few of these publications are:

The Atlantic Auto Advertiser, P.O. Box 70, Kingston, Massachusetts 02360
Cars & Parts, 114 East Franklin Avenue, P.O. Box 299, Sesser, Illinois 62884
Hemmings Motor News, P.O. Box 433, Quincy, Illinois 62301
The Restorers Automart, P.O. Box 6293, Marietta, Georgia 30062
Spoke Wheels, 3735 Ector Street, Beaumont, Texas 77705

The growing list of Floyd Clymer Publications includes reprints of manuals. A copy of the current catalogue may be obtained from: Floyd Clymer Publications, 222 No. Virgil Avenue, Los Angeles, California 90004.

The mail-order catalogues of Sears, Roebuck and of Montgomery, Ward should not be overlooked, as they advertise many Model A and Model T Ford parts.

INDEX

INDEX

INDEX